Machine Learning

Learning

Develop Machine Learning Tools and Techniques

(Deep Learning Models a Programmer's Guide to Artificial Intelligence)

Charles Brown

Published By **Bella Frost**

Charles Brown

Machine Learning: Develop Machine Learning Tools and Techniques (Deep Learning Models a Programmer's Guide to Artificial Intelligence)

ISBN   978-0-9959965-9-5

Legal & Disclaimer

Table Of Contents

Chapter 1: What Are Machine Learning And Artificial Intelligence?

How an Algorithm Works

To understand what machine learning is we first must know what an algorithm is and how it works. Most programming is actually based off of mathematics and it is thanks to a man called Turing that we have computers in the first place. Turing built a state reserved system or rather a system that preserved and used the current state of the system in order to do calculations. Most of this is unknown to the public beyond the fact that it was this machine that helped to break the famous German Enigma codes during World War II. Algorithms come from mathematics and this is the reason why we are able to translate algorithms into programming languages because programming languages are based on mathematics. Therefore, the more mathematics you know, the stronger your programming skills are likely going to be.

An algorithm, or a function, represents a step by step process on how to take inputs or variables and turn them into output or result variables. The term variable represents the fact that the data inside of the variable is changing or can be changed. Result variables are results that are changing or can be changed, which is why a having a state preserved machine is so important when it comes to programming. In programming, a function will take in variables and make decisions on it before it either returns more variables based on those decisions or provides your final output. This is how, conceptually, algorithms work inside of programs. This is the core of how machine learning works.

How a Recursive Algorithm Works

Whenever we talk about recursive algorithms, we are talking about algorithms that call on themselves until they get to the desired result. The primary example utilized for this is the Fibonacci code. You have to continuously call on the function in order to produce a series of numbers that will ultimately give you the Fibonacci code. However, since the Fibonacci code can be somewhat complex and confusing for most individuals, I have found that I often have a better chance of showing what a recursive algorithm is by simply working through a string. Since a string is literally a set of ASCII characters that have been displayed using a reference format, you can iterate through them much like you could elements inside of what is known as an array, which is like a grocery list. Below, you will find a recursive algorithm that iterates through a single string but calls on itself each time it needs to go to the next character.

Neural Networks

A neural network, the hard-coded machine behind the concept of machine learning, is a series of if statements that can be as big as you want them to be but ultimately handle the feature of the problem that you want to solve. Most of the time, these neural networks are designed to handle complex features that require severe amounts of processing power in order to complete them, such as recognizing faces or the products that they are searching for inside of an image. With a neural network, you have inputs (such as a massive amount of data that you would normally not be able to search through on your own), you have your neural network (which represents the different markers that you are looking for inside of that data), and finally you have what is known as your output as a result of this data.

Recursive Neural Networks

Just as you saw with the recursive algorithm that I displayed for you, neural networks can also be applied in a recursive manner. The reason you would want to do that is something called the fading gradient. This refers to the fact that data can get so complex and neural networks can have so many connections, that the neural network itself is what slows down the overall process and makes it worse than a regular algorithm. Normally, this creates a problem for any type of machine learning that requires anything more than three layers of neural nodes. The reason recursive neural networks were created was because of the concept of convoluted neural networks, which we will talk about later on.

Essentially, each neural node is connected to the neural nodes that came before it. Therefore, whenever you have a neural node on the network and you have three layers of neural nodes on that network with one node per layer (so you would have 3 and 1 layer and then 3 in the second layer). You need to take into consideration that it is a factor of x every time you go to the next node in the node network. Therefore, if you start out at the first node, you are only connected to one node. However, when that node goes to the next node in the neural network, that next node will have 3 nodes connected to it. When it goes to the next node in the network, it will have 9 nodes connected to it. When it goes to the next node in the network, it will have 81 nodes connected to it. The next node will have 6,561 nodes and then that next will have 43,046,721 and then that next will have 1,853,020,188,851,841. As you can see, this number gets extremely huge extremely fast and massive neural networks simply aren't possible without recursive algorithms to slim down the number of neural network nodes that are connected together.

What is Machine Learning?

Machine learning is literally the process of everything I just described above with the addition of utilizing a decision tree which we will talk about later. Essentially, the data goes in one section and gets filtered through the different neural nodes on the neural network to produce a result on the other end of the network. If that result is not what is expected, we then look at the neural network to see if any problems occurred. If no problems occurred inside of the network then we know that the data set might either be bad, or we may not have considered all of the variables. On the other hand, if the neural network is incorrect then we add what are known as biases and weights so that we can get closer to the answer (this may need to happen several times to get the expected result). This is the learning part of machine learning whereas the machine part is the fact that a machine is doing it.

What is AI?

AI, otherwise known as Artificial Intelligence, is not the same thing as machine learning, and I find it very frustrating that people seem to confuse the two. Although machine learning is a form of AI, it is not the only form of AI. Artificial intelligence is the ability to fake intelligence. Video games have been doing this for decades because first-person shooters need enemies that can provide them with a challenge. In video games, this artificial intelligence is represented by what is known as a field of view variable where if a person's X & Y coordinates are within a certain radius from the enemies' X & Y radius, then the enemy automatically moves towards the person's coordinates. Additionally, if they are within x amount of range then the enemy character starts attacking and doing damage regardless of whether they would logically be able to do damage in real life if they were facing that position. This creates a sense that the enemy can kill the player because they are intelligent, but it has only simulated the intelligence that we have ourselves.

Machine learning, on the other hand, performs tasks that make it seem like the machine is intelligent, but the machine is only capable of doing that task because we took time to tweak algorithms to get it to that exact result. It's kind of like saying that a spear is intelligent because it never fails to pierce flesh but if we were to try to use a spear for anything else, it would be difficult if not completely impossible. The same is said of an image recognition machine that seems intelligent until you try to apply it to crunch the stock market numbers. It is faked intelligence that seems to be intelligent to us.

Chapter 2: What Is A Predictive Model? What Do The Scores Represent?

What is a Predictive Model?

A predictive model is a model that takes in information and makes a prediction based on the data that has been given to it. In fact, there is an entire industry based on predictive models called statistics. We would not have statistics if we weren't interested in predictive models because statistics do the same thing but on a much more manual level. A predictive model looks at the data and generates a mathematical formula that will help you to predict what is likely going to happen at different future time intervals based on the information that it is handed. You can do this with statistics, but you would have to do it by hand whereas predictive modeling is usually done by the computer.

What is the human equivalent of the Predictive Model?

The human equivalent of the predictive model is most noticeable in your local weatherman because your local weatherman uses a predictive model all the time. They feed the collected data into a predictive model to try and predict what it's going to be like over the next X amount of days. Organizations also do this whenever they are attempting to see when crime is rising or falling, detect when situations may be getting out of hand, and when business revenues seem to be going up by most of the numbers but through predictive modeling you can figure out that sometimes the numbers can be deceiving as we will see in the next chapter. It is important to know that predictive models are forms of neural networks that have been pre-designed to predict equations based off of linear data and so you may need a different solution if you have nonlinear data.

What do the scores represent?

The two most known predictive models are nonparametric and parametric models. Parametric models assume that you know where one of the parameters is causing most of the change in your data, and so nonparametric data represents one that you don't know where it is. Nearly all neural networks that are out there on the market can be utilized in a way that provides you with a predictive model, but those are the two most common types of models inside of the predictive model genre. The scoring inside of a predictive model is really representative of what you're trying to do with the predictive model. For example, a credit card company could set up a scoring system with a predictive model that judges the successfulness of an individual to be able to pay for the credit that they loan them based off of their past transaction history.

Where are Predictive Models Used?

Predictive models are used whenever you are talking about applications, simply because it works wherever anything can be predicted. Some examples are crime rates, financial decisions, work performance, and the list really goes on for where this type of neural network can be used. In fact, it is used on a daily basis to not only tell you what the weather is, but it will also be used to run the traffic lights in major cities to ensure that there are less rush hour traffic accidents, and to determine the likelihood that an area will be affected by current traffic models. The list really does go on when it comes to predictive models and where they are used.

USING A PREDICTIVE MODEL TO MAKE DECISIONS

Gathering Data

Let's say that you have decided to use some predictive modeling software, but you don't see the true benefits of it. After all, no machine can truly be that good at predicting the future to where this is such a vital tool, right? The first step is that we collect our data and let's say that our data looks something like this.

Taking a Guess At It

Now, it's obvious I'm doing my standard programming here, but I want you to take a stab at guessing what the next few numbers will be. What, difficult? Yeah, it should be because you just see a bunch of numbers. But you should also see that we receive a base revenue of 22 for some reason, so that should help. What, you can't think of one? Well, to be honest, I didn't expect you to because all you see is a ton of numbers and it is difficult to tell what the correlation between them might be. If we were to just guess on what's going to happen just based off of revenue, we could say we might see an increase, but we are more or less going to see the chart go down one for the next to and rise by a few points for every third one.

However, as you will see, this could prove erroneous.

Noticing the massive change

There are a number of software solutions out there for you but in order to create this environment, I needed to make sure that I had full control over both ends so I programmed this in by hand. What would normally happen is you would have a spreadsheet of numbers, such as a csv, and this would then be fed into the software that would produce a prediction as well as the exact algorithm it used to achieve that prediction. I already have that algorithm on hand.

As we can see, this equation is simplistic by nature, but let's see what the full sheet looks like:

What we now see is that not only does the revenue stagnate, but in the last week, this ultimately results in a significant drop in revenue. I say that this is significant because it drops below the point where we first began to feed data into the system. Imagine if you had made an even worse prediction in a real-world environment! If you hadn't used a predictive model, you would be telling your bosses or yourself that you would expect revenue to have a slow rise when you would actually see a massive drop. Image if this were in the millions. $6 isn't much but $6,000,000 is a ton of lost revenue and this was a good scenario, something that wouldn't ultimately cause people to lose jobs.

A Short message from the Author:

Hey, are you enjoying the book? I'd love to hear your thoughts!

Many readers do not know how hard reviews are to come by, and how much they help an author.

I would be incredibly thankful if you could take just 60 seconds to write a brief review on Amazon, even if it's just a few sentences!

>> Click here to leave a quick review

Thank you for taking the time to share your thoughts!

Your review will genuinely make a difference for me and help gain exposure for my work.

Chapter 3: What Are Decision Trees?

How a Program Works

Decisions trees are very similar to programming, and how a singular program works can be sufficiently complicated enough. For a program, you must first write the code in order for the program to start up with all the necessary variables. Then, the code is based on how the user will interact with the program, and sometimes there are multiple levels of IF statements that help control the flow of functionality for the user so that the user just isn't looking at a giant list of functions that they can use without some guidance on how to use them. You might think of Photoshop as a good example because Photoshop has a section called filters where you have a selection of different types of filters that do different types of things but all of them are sorted into subcategories that you can choose sub-items from. Now, the only problem is that a program only makes a decision based off of the user input and so as much as you may be nesting all of the complexity of the logic, you are still waiting on the user to make the final decision in this puzzle.

How You Make Decisions as a Person

The honest truth is that you use decision trees all the time, but you don't realize it because you utilize it as a natural process. Decision trees are really good at breaking things down whenever you have multiple choices and you need to decide the best choice in that case. Normally, you can make a decision tree graph that will help you make a relatively uncomplicated choice such as what type of application development you want to undertake or what type of television show you want to watch. You make these decisions without the conscious use of a decision tree because most of the time our brain has already gone through the decision tree at that point. This is because we are accustomed to needing to make decisions within a few seconds to a few minutes until our brains naturally break things down into if statements, which is why we have them inside of our programming, so that the brain can then deduce whether it wants to go with one decision, another decision, and so on and so forth. Whenever you make a decision tree, you are simply elaborating on the flow that it took you to get to such a decision, but you leave out the decision because it is up to the computer to get to that decision based off of what's inside of the decision tree.

How a Decision Tree is Made

There are three components to the most basic of decision trees. You have decision nodes that take you to the next label or feature, the root node/label that starts everything, and, finally, the leaf nodes that represent your results based on your decision nodes.

The Ultimate Goal of a Decision Tree

The ultimate goal of a decision tree is a two-part goal depending on what you are hoping to achieve with the tree. The first part is that if you are planning to have your tree come out with some ultimate result that matches a correct answer, then the ultimate goal is to get a decision tree that is capable of taking large quantities of inputs and giving the correct output most of the time. On the other hand, if you are doing the second part, and that is feeding data in to hopefully create a decision tree that can give you some sort of result that you don't know yet, then the ultimate goal is to whittle the unnecessary information down to the point where you can extract useful information at usable quantities. This is the ultimate goal of the decision tree and it really matches how we work as human beings.

Let us take a survival situation as an example. Whenever you make a decision as a person in a survival situation you are either making the decision based on an outcome you previously saw, an emergency manual that you hope will hold true, or you are just using the information that is the most useful to you at the time to make an ultimate decision, otherwise known as an educated guess. As you can see, a neural network is very similar to how an actual brain works and so you can utilize it to conquer many of the things that the brain naturally does but at the speed of a machine.

NEURAL NETWORKS AND DEEP LEARNING

Some Types of Neural Networks

Feedforward

Feed-forward networks are really simple to understand because they simply mean networks that you put information into so that it can go in a linear direction represented as forward inside of the network. This was the first type of neural network ever developed before we began using something known as backpropagation.

Autoencoder

An autoencoder is rather weird whenever you describe it to the average individual because the purpose of this type of neural network is to feed it input so that it can break that input apart and see if it can put the input back together. This is the most famous type of neural network when it comes to unsupervised learning because you don't really need to keep an eye on it and feed it data that is specifically geared towards beginning steps. You just feed it data and see if it gets the correct data out again and change it if it doesn't.

Probabilistic

This type of network is usually utilized for pattern recognition and it actually has four different layers; it has an input layer, pattern layer, summation layer, and an output layer. The pattern layer relies on the radial basis function to determine the distance of your current test case from the neural node by utilizing the sigma values. The summation layer serves as a hidden layer that will help summarize which category the pattern best fits into per case. The reason why this type of network exists is that it's usually faster than the beginning neural networks that we used to have such as multi-layer perceptron networks, and is a lot more accurate when it comes to predictions and excluding any outliers.

Time Delay

If you have live data coming forward and you need to feed it immediately into a neural network, the time delay neural network is built for this type of data. The way a time delay neural network works is that it usually a has a perceptron network that has been developed by using back propagated connection weights and it forcibly delays the amount of time that it takes a specific neural node to give an output.

Convolutional

A convolutional neural network is currently the most popular type of neural network that's out there for machine learning. What it does is utilize the concept of convolution, which is where you utilize two separate functions to figure out what you need for a third function to work or to be generated from those two functions. There's a lot of applications that utilize the convolutional concept of a neural network. You know it for image and video recognition, but it's also used in Google Voice as well as any systems that might be recommending something to you.

RNN

The most common type of neural network that's out there is the recurrent-neural-network. There are several different forms that this neural network can take but the principle aspects of this type of neuron that work are really easy to understand. This is a feed forward type of network that can go backward at certain steps to reprocess information. The most common example of where we use this is our spelling correction programs that look at previous words in the sentence to determine if that word is incorrectly spelled or grammatically incorrect.

Modular

A modular neural network is a neural network that's made up of several other different neural networks. The reason why you might want to have this is if you need text recognition on top of image recognition in the same neural network to analyze a single picture. There are several reasons why you might want to combine these networks and there are several different types of modular networks. However, they all follow the same definition as being a network of other smaller neural networks.

The True Meaning Behind Deep Learning

There seems to be this mystique behind deep learning that a lot of people fantasize about, but deep learning is a really simple concept and is nowhere near as mystical as is made out to be. Deep learning simply means that the neural network that you are working with has more than one layer of neural nodes to it to further increase the amount of machine learning that is occurring. In fact, the full name for deep learning is deep machine learning. The reason why it represents more than one layer of neural nodes is that the information goes deeper into the neural network in order to produce the results that you are looking for. We developers really need to think about the names that we label things because the same thing happened

27

whenever computers came around and people were somewhat afraid of touching them. Now we have Terminator references popping up again.

Chapter 4: How To Use Decision Trees

Using Digit Representation

It's important to realize right off the bat that a computer does not recognize the words yes and no. Instead, we computer scientists have come up with the clever trick of using 1 for yes and 0 for no. The reason this is important is that all your features and your output results are going to be represented as numbers and not anything that would normally be recognizable to the human eyes such as a literal answer to your question. Similar to the reason why the answer to life is 42, we must first recognize that the computer is not going to be able to speak in sentences unless you're building that type of network, and then, of course, it will be able to speak in sentences, but that doesn't mean it'll speak in sentences that you can understand at first. Instead, you need to have a numerical representation of every output that you plan to have. So, if you were to have 6 different types of output then you would choose maybe the numbers 2 through 8 since 0 and 1 represent true and false, or yes and no.

Choose Your Desired Outputs if Possible

Some of us are without the benefit of a desired output so sometimes the output is just a random jumble of numbers that we need to make sense of. But most of us require that a machine learning algorithm actually do something that we want it to do. For instance, a good machine learning algorithm is the facial recognition machine learning algorithm. The end goal was to detect faces inside of images, so all our output would be a square around where the image was but in the form of numbers. Therefore, the lower numbers represented areas that didn't likely have a face inside of it whereas the higher numbers represented an area where there was likely a face in it. As I already said before, machine learning algorithms are designed to work with numbers and not literal items unless we are talking about big machine learning algorithms that took months to develop such as the convolutional deep neural network. This is the type of network that Facebook currently uses in order to detect the faces inside of our pictures.

The Main Decision Gets the Ball Rolling: Root Node

The first thing that I'm going to do is I'm going to generate a bunch of random numbers so that we have a data set to work with. I am not entirely sure what our data set is going to give us but I'm going to make the decision to filter out most of the results and this is what is known as the root node. Here is the algorithm to generate this dataset of random numbers between 1-100:

Now, I will not show the numbers of the dataset because it would take up a ton of space when I don't need to take that space. However, I believe our root node is going to filter out whether the number is below fifty or above fifty. I'm going to refrain using complex Ruby code here simply because I know that most Data Science is done in Python and R, I just like Ruby. This is what the code is for making the root node as well as the result:

Why did I leave the first two open? No real reason. What you will learn in Data Science is that you want to have as much data as possible going in and coming out so having a larger result array is usually preferable.

Nodes in Your "Network": Making Decisions

Bias

Adding a bias to the system is similar to adding a weight to the system but it represents a different aspect of the system. Whenever you are introducing a bias to the system that means that you know that the results are likely going to be wrong. In the method that we have up here, we don't need to add a bias.

But if we were to do something like image detection or something much more complicated where we don't actually know that we are just dealing with random numbers, then we would likely use a bias so that as we recursively developed our machine learning algorithm, we could change the biases to effectively bring the result closer or further from the expected result by changing the bias and utilizing the bias in the final calculation. The goal is to have a very simple equation that allows you to get a number and then based on the importance of that node, we want a certain bias from that node to affect the result. This is why almost all biases start off with a null or 0 value so that they don't affect anything before you begin to change things. When you get an outcome that you didn't expect, you go through the biases and see which one of the nodes would have likely caused that inappropriate outcome to happen and change the bias to see if you can get that node to give you the correct outcome. Most of the time, you will not be changing the core logic of each of the nodes but rather the bias and the weights of the nodes.

Weights

The weight of a node really just represents the importance of that node in the neural network. If you have important data that you want to utilize immediately then you put it in the important node area, which is why different nodes have different weights. Additionally, biases and weights allow you to keep track of where data is traveling in the neural network so that when something unexpected happens you can look back at the results of the weights and the biases to see where it could have possibly gone wrong.

Feature

A feature represents the logic behind a specific node or collection of nodes. When we implemented the logic of testing to see if our number was below or above 50, we created a feature that described the value of the number. Features represent important questions you want to ask about the data to get the ultimate outcome that you are expecting or that you hope will occur. I'm going to go ahead and add some additional logic and the goal for my code is to test whether the numbers in our array are truly random.

Getting Results: Leaf Nodes

Now that we have most of the logic done for this extremely basic non-biased non-weighted neural network, we need to make our final decision. A final decision is made in a similar manner, but it has two overall components. The Confidence variable represents just how sure the program is of the prediction that it is making, while the Prediction is the actual True or False Decision of the program. Therefore, we are going to add one more open element to our results array and use the first two elements in the array to provide a Random or Not Random result. We'll go ahead and move this into its own separate method.

Now, as you can see, we got a Random Variable back with 100% confidence. However, since I know that I used a Random function, I know that my machine learning algorithm is wrong. There could be several areas where I did something wrong. For instance, my decision nodes have several things wrong with them, or holes if you will.

1. Do I really need to divide everything in half? This is a useless step.

2. Will there always be a definite case where the number is definitely going to be both below or above the second result if I add my bias? It would be more likely if I put an "or" there.

There may be some additional bad logic in there, but I'm going to fix what I see and show you the array.

Suddenly, by changing the code to fix some of the bugs not only did I get a correct answer, but I am also aware that if I use "or", then either one or both cases could be true, and this could be problematic. However, since I got a positive result here, I would generate another random array to test that array and if it was wrong then I would change the logic, bias, and confidence even further. So, as you can see, this is not only how you make a decision tree but also how you start a neural network. This one just so happens to be testing whether or not something is random.

Making it Look Nice

Up until this point, we have been looking at an array, but this is what the data scientist will see and if you have more categories then you likely do not want to be stuck looking at some numbers on the screen. Therefore, you may choose to print something out like this:

So, why should we do this? Well, for one, it allows us to visualize the data much better and to understand our final results. Additionally, if we see something odd then we'll be able to see it immediately like this. Finally, we do this for people who are not us and do not understand arrays.

Chapter 5: How To Use Big Data For Business

Precise Marketing

Let us say that we are a coffee shop that sells coffee in New York City. Do we really want to advertise our coffee across the nation, or do we just want to advertise our coffee to the people of New York City in a fashion that only the people of New York City would be able to understand? Machine learning is capable of acquiring the living areas where individuals who purchase your product currently reside, and where the majority of individuals that buy your products are located. Never before have we been able to collect this type of data so quickly and so readily because people often have no problem giving out their address to companies who develop applications for instantly paying at the location they are buying from. The reason why this is important is that marketing has begun to evolve over the past two decades. National television, television that usually was either carried over cable television or radio towers that sent out free channels, charges a massive fee for advertisements to be displayed on the television nationally. When something like YouTube came out, we started to gain access to advertisements in a localized area such as the United States of America, rather than Canada or Mexico, which could have been utilizing the television network as it expanded into other countries and didn't only include cable television and free channels via radio signals. Once we started getting access to regional advertising, Facebook began to localize the advertisement to specific individuals who fit categories that we wanted to advertise to. Google, once again, took this even further by localizing the advertisements to the neighborhoods that we wanted to advertise to.

Machine learning has the potential to take the next step in this evolution by analyzing the customers in your database along with the provided addresses to figure out exactly which houses buy the most amount of product from you, and which houses buy some product but could buy more product. As you can already see, having such knowledge would give you access to the people you primarily want to advertise to, that you are likely to see the most success with the least amount of cost. Businesses spend millions of dollars on advertising, and as we have seen through the sponsorships on YouTube, marketing has become cheaper and cheaper as people with giant audiences don't mind agreeing to smaller amounts of money to advertise a product to a category of people.

Product Creation

As our machines get more complicated and our technical parts become so complicated that it is difficult for an organization to create most of those parts, machine learning takes a step forward by being able to crunch the numbers that we, as humans, are not capable of crunching. A good example of this is the quantum computer that was developed a while back and is now solving some of the biggest problems in our history because regular computing simply can't perform the tasks of these calculations at the speed at which Quantum Computing can. The problem is that we don't all have access to Quantum Computing. That doesn't mean that if we had access to Quantum Computing it would be useful to us.

Machine learning is all about mimicking the human mind and finding a way for the usefulness of the human mind to run at the speed of the computer mind. When we develop new products through upgrades, we must make design and engineering choices based on what can provide the best upgrades. These choices are mathematically broken down into specific sciences that one can study and develop to create enhancements that are very alluring.

Remember that if a machine can study a certain area by using mathematics, such as the ones that I just mentioned, it can do the job better and faster given enough examples and development time. This suggests that future smartphones and other products that require a specialist viewpoint might be created by machine learning rather than an individual simply because the requirement to develop these machines is so high that only machines are capable of conceptualizing them without any help from others.

Feature Selection

When we talk about features as normal human beings, we are talking about items that make up an entity, and we are technically talking about the same thing whenever it comes to machine learning. However, when we talk about features inside of software development we are often talking about special tools that the user can use in order to get some type of task done.

A good example of this is Photoshop because Photoshop has a ton of features. One of the features of Photoshop is that you can crop images so that you can remove any unwanted background from an image whether it is with a box crop or if it is selecting the background through exact precision. This would normally be considered a feature of the program and the honest truth is that a lot of time is spent in developing these features because these features ultimately determine the user experience that an individual has inside of an application. Hundreds of hours are spent on upgrading software so that it has the newest features that you can possibly have to create the best user experience that it can possibly provide. Needless to say, if you hand over the information about the largest number of complaints that a user base has about a piece of software, and the largest number of requests from a company to develop certain features, you can shorten the amount of work needed to figure out which features should be in the new upgrade so that more time can be spent on making those features. However, in a very scary sense of the word, we can also develop these features using machine learning. If a machine learns how to code a feature, then it is possible for a machine to learn how to get the end result we are looking for out of that feature and then provide us with the necessary code to insert into our program. This is scary because it essentially replaces the need for any type of web developer, software developer, and pretty much anyone that isn't a data scientist. That is a lot of people. We are talking about nearly half the higher education job force.

Locate Issues Before They Become Massive

I suppose the last benefit that comes out of machine learning is that you can locate your issues before they become a massive problem. This is the case if you have developed a machine learning algorithm correctly. There is a quality assurance process known as Six-Sigma that allows companies to track down problematic situations causing the productive workflow of an environment to slow down. If a machine learning algorithm were to be taught the Six-Sigma techniques, and were to successfully implement a Six-Sigma environment so that it can begin measuring the different variables, we can now say that we would have program that could effectively track down a problem causing instance before it became big enough for us to notice. The reason why this is beneficial is that it helps to prevent things like salmonella poisoning, worker injuries, and a ton of other problems that come with the physical manufacturing and inspection of products. Additionally, the products that we would produce would actually increase and so a company would be able to sell more and thus gain more profit as a result of having a machine learning algorithm that was capable of maximizing the productivity range of the environment that they've been deployed to.

NEW TECHNOLOGIES IN MACHINE LEARNING

Machine Learning in Games

Developers over in the Asian countries have begun to place machine learning inside of their games because machine learning offers the capability to enrich the game experience by simulating actual conversation. While the size of the deep-learning network is small (because you would have to deal with the volume of players that are online at any given time so the calculations would be out of this world) these conversations are primarily centered around providing a natural feeling to the conversation a player is having with an NPC, and additionally finds new ways to entice their consumers into purchasing additional content that they like based off of their interactions with the neural network. This has a significant impact with things like customer service and sheds light on an almost entirely new industry with machine learning because now consumers can provide producers with a much better understanding about what they want out of the producer company.

Sophia: AI Workers in a new Light

Sofia is a robot that is so sophisticatedly built that Saudi Arabia granted Sofia citizenship. The dilemma behind Sophia is one of the few different key points that is currently affecting Saudi Arabia. Of course, the very first thing that a lot of people don't like about this action is that Saudi Arabia already has problems with giving rights to women. A woman has to be with a man if they are to give a public speech, and several other rules apply simply out of sexism because they believe that a woman is incapable of being on her own. The reason Sofia is a problem here is because Sophia seems to have more rights, and because she looks like a woman, they automatically judge her based off of her appearance rather than based off of what she is, which is a robot. However, it also brings into perspective the possibility that AI may no longer be machines that simply do one task, but are capable of doing multiple tasks and have citizenship. This brings up the question as to whether an AI should be paid for the work that it does, and it blurs the line between Robotics and Humanity.

Social Media Responses

A few companies in the past year have learned why you should always test something before you decide to use it, as they have begun to develop machine learning so that more accurate audience targeting social media messages can be sent out over social media networks, essentially replacing the need for a social media manager. The job of a social media manager is to study the business and the social feeds along with their interactions to see how they should interact with the audience of that social media account. These new machine learning algorithms suggest that it is possible to remove this job and represents a new product that companies can sell to each other when it comes to marketing by having more advanced machine learning algorithms provide better responses to consumers interacting with the business through social media applications.

Development of Materials Fabrication and Processes

Part of the problem with creating new materials in this day in age is the amount of research that needs to go into creating them in the first place. You see, when a new material needs to be created, the normal way to do this is to scour the academic journals to learn how other similar materials were made, and determine if there were any missing combinations of components that can be used to develop the new materials, and the process to develop them. It takes, potentially, hundreds of hours just to find a new material and then an equal or slightly less amount of time to develop a new process to make that material. MIT is putting together a machine learning algorithm that will search through all the digitized forms of research to not only suggest materials to be made, but also the process in which to make them.

FeatureHub by MIT

Another addition to the machine learning community is the addition of a tool utilized by MIT. This tool will allow machine learning enthusiasts to develop features for other machine learning scientists. Let us say that you are having difficulty coming up with features for a current problem that you were dealing with but the old methods of creating features with the help of others required that you go to each one individually and hope that they didn't also want to do the project. Now, the tool that MIT provides will allow individuals to go onto a website and submit their problems so that other machine learning scientists can suggest features for them to utilize or options on how to solve the problem. This is a first for machine learning scientists.

Azure and Amazon AI

One problem that has cropped up for many of those who would like to participate in the active machine learning community is the amount of processing power that is required to perform large-scale data processing. These require huge machines that cost a lot of money, but most scientists are not rich, especially if those scientists are either just coming out of school or are hobbyists. As a solution to this answer, Microsoft and Amazon have both created their own products to provide the capability of machine learning. Microsoft has created an Azure machine that can allow you to quickly formulate a decision tree for your neural network to go through and visualize that decision tree in the same action. Amazon, on the other hand, is a little bit more open-minded by providing a platform that gives you the hardware. but not the actual tools that you are working on. The primary choice is to utilize Tensor Flow, but you also have access to Frameworks of your choosing such as torch, theano, and Cafe 2.

Chapter 6: Ethical Use Of Machine Learning For Business

Minority Consideration

Whenever we develop any type of machine learning or any type of algorithm for that matter in America, we also tend to only account for the white individuals of the population simply because they make up most of the population. Now, I'm not here to say whether this is going to be true going into the future, but the problem is that we develop our systems based off of this imaginary bias. The problem with only utilizing white individuals as the basis for our calculations is that it doesn't take in the minority as a consideration, and this is true of developing anything with the bias of either a Christian or a Muslim because these two religions make up the majority of the religions in the world. By not taking into consideration the minority individuals in the world, we begin to make machines that have holes in them. A good example is the debacle that Google had a little while ago with its learning machine because women had an extraordinarily high amount of search queries for black individuals. Because Google didn't account for the persistent problem that the black community has with jail time and being persecuted by the police, Google began suggesting background searches and police searches whenever the search was related towards male individuals who were also black. This led to several hurtful, hilarious, but also troublesome titles that would say that the Google search algorithm was racist because they suggested the background and jail time searches for black men. Technically, you could also say that that was sexist, but you can't really say that the political discourse at that time was too concerned with sexism.

Now, why is such an aspect important when it comes to developing machine learning for businesses? Well, the truth is that when businesses develop machine learning it's usually to handle a process that's very massive in its size and scope. An example might be trying to recruit individuals online. If you are looking for a personality that matches more towards white individuals than black individuals, or you are searching through an industry that is usually full of white individuals more than black individuals, then the data that you feed it will begin recording the traits of the two different groups. But since you gave it more of one race than the other, it is a possibility that the machine could learn to only associate the good qualities with the white individuals of the data set that you provided. This is just a small example of how not including minorities as an equal part of the test can eventually disrupt the correct answers you're looking for inside of the machine learning.

Guessing Accuracy

It may be convenient to utilize machine learning in a situation where the answer needs to be the best answer based off of data and the data is so big that your average scientists can't digest it all before you need to make a decision. A good example is if a mudslide is occurring or if a tornado is in the area and you need answers very quickly. In terms of business, a better answer to this type of example would be if you need to make a decision on whether it is a good idea to open up to the public or to stay a private company, or even whether you want to sell a certain product in a very controversial market. It is increasingly important to make sure that the guesses that you get out of machine learning are accurate guesses because when you rely on machine learning to give you numbers to cover the market, you want a general sense of correctness in those numbers. If your machine learning is ever used to do anything important, you want to make sure that you have taken the steps to give your neural network as many correct answers as it can possibly digest so that you know that your machine learning algorithm is giving you the correct choices. While some of the examples I used would mean that you would profit from getting the best correct answers, you also have to realize that in a case where machine learning is used to tackle a very large and vast problem, you would want to make sure that you were making the correct choice based off of the correct data, such as in the case of firing an employee because the employee might be the reason why your company is not being as productive as it could be, or they could very well not be. Let's say that you have a thousand employees on staff and you noticed that the productivity levels have significantly decreased over the past week. You have an idea of who it could be, but you want to use machine learning to look at all the variables and see what machine learning gives you before you decide to fire the employee because the employee fulfills a role that is difficult to replace. Therefore, you begin trying to design this learning machine to figure out how you could pinpoint the source of a problem and who is responsible for the tasks that are not being taken care of. However, because you have an idea of who it is, you begin changing the algorithm to pinpoint the reason why you think it might that be that individual. Suddenly, your machine learning algorithm is saying that it is correct because it has detected all the external biases you have put into the machine. In this case, your belief that a specific somebody was the result of the problems in your company caused you to create a learning machine algorithm that would only target that type of person, rather than target the actual person who might be causing the problem. This means that you used the learning machine to fire an individual that doesn't need to be fired and so next week, when you notice that you have the same problem, you won't know what went wrong because you'll think that your machine was designed correctly and that you made the correct decision, even though you fired an individual based off of a machine that was designed to pinpoint that individual and not provide an accurate guess.

Developer Bias

This actually brings me to my next topic because whoever develops the machine learning is going to have certain biases whenever it comes to choosing the data. For instance, they may not be particularly racist, but they could only choose black individuals as their dataset or they could choose only white individuals as their data set without even realizing that they're doing this. It is vitally important that you always make sure that the individuals that are making your learning machine are of separate backgrounds because we all have our individual vices and underlying biases that affect how we implement systems. If we don't take into account the fact that we are all different, then we end up with systems that exclude the individuals who are different. It is important for not only those who are going to be affected by this machine learning algorithm to have a part in it and to have a say in it; but also to reflect on to you and what it is going to do for you.

Delegating Proper Priorities

It is vitally important for the entire system that develops this machine learning algorithm to realize that the entire picture is important and that the variables that you were looking at are not the deciding factor of the system. A lot of people who set out to develop a machine learning algorithm ultimately are setting out to develop a system to detect one item but what you need to realize is that if you set out to detect one item then you're going to miss the big picture and sometimes, as a result of narrowing your viewpoint, you actually miss some of the factors that would help you target what you want to target. This is why it's very important to clearly define what your system is going to do by looking at the big picture rather than a very narrow and selective set of information. When you go through something like supervised machine learning, you are teaching it to gradually get better and better at getting the end result that you want. But if the result that you want only takes into account one specific thing, then it is likely that some information that is important to that one specific thing will get lost across the journey that the data has to take. By setting a very clear goal and by ensuring that your machine learning algorithm takes in the larger picture, it can accommodate for the greatest number of issues so as to make a machine that is more robust and capable of handling more than that one thing should you decide to expand its uses.

Digital to Physical Implementation Impact

Let us say that you developed a machine learning algorithm that removes the need to write down material. There is absolutely no need for anyone to write any more after you create this machine learning algorithm. Better yet, let's just go ahead and expand on this and ensure that no one would need to schedule anything anymore because you have created an application that is capable of listening to your wants and scheduling them perfectly. Not only that, but it can take all of your files and organize them for you and call people to set up meetings. Now that we've created this awesome machine learning algorithm, what happens to all of the secretaries in the world? A secretary is supposed to write things down, be able to follow the individual who they work for, schedule meetings and call people to set up those meetings, and finally, organize the files. This machine that you have developed will essentially replace the need for having a secretary and since having a secretary is usually a luxury, we can't really say that a secretary is absolutely vital or a special skill in most cases. Therefore, not only is the position not absolutely vital to run a company but you can also avoid paying an individual for the spot of being a secretary because you can have a machine do it. In fact, this is something that happened whenever several scheduling applications came out that could also pull up personal files. The truth of the matter is that while we may not have replaced all secretaries, there was a significant impact because we created a technology that did somebody else's job. Additionally, a secretarial position doesn't have anything it can translate into unless you want to add some extra skills on to it, and so all of the secretaries that were fired because an application was capable of doing their job had to go into different fields of work in order to compensate for their lack of a job. Some of these secretaries had been doing their job for nearly two decades.

Now we are even thinking about automating truck driving using driverless trucks, all the truckers on the road that normally earned anywhere from $15 to $20 an hour will be out of a job with only trucking as their experience. This is another job that represents a position that doesn't translate very well into other positions and that if we replace them, thousands of individuals will be out of work.

This is something that a lot of people are pointing out and the fact of the matter is that when you decide to utilize digital tools to impact physical performance, you need to make sure that the impact that you are going to have is a good one more than it is a negative one. Replacing the thousands of individuals who would normally have a job with a robot simply because it costs a company less is not exactly an ethical decision. This means that whenever we provide a digital solution, we also need to think over the physical impact that solution might have if we were to introduce it to the world on a mass scale so that we can handle the ramifications.

Turing Ethics

The case of Sophia brings up a very interesting point inside of computer science and machine learning because Sophia is the first robot to receive citizenship in the world. I often tell people that the reason why Sophia received citizenship, beyond the advertisement of Saudi Arabia as a technology hub in the world, was also to prevent possible problems that one could come across, ethically, with developing these AI systems. If you have ever watched any futuristic movie that had a dark theme to it but also included robots that were capable of human interaction, then the usual side joke would be that men would have access to robotic women that would provide services that normal women would not provide. The truth of the matter is that if we treated these systems as tools and gadgets rather than the potential sentient beings that they might become, we might honestly turn this fantasy into reality. I'm not saying that this is a particularly bad thing but, at the same time, if you are a married individual and your particular religion says that you cannot commit adultery, but you have intercourse with a robot, does this count as adultery? Is robotic prostitution any different than actual prostitution? We often see robots as tools that are designed to help us, but we also have carnal desires and a lot of individuals see advanced robotics as a solution to the rejection of others. Now that Sofia is a citizen, she is protected by law from acts of adultery and similar cruel experiments that would be performed on machines that are not performed on humans. Her citizenship prevents the people working on her from doing anything to her that would not normally be done to a citizen of Saudi Arabia. Like I said, her situation is very interesting because it brings up a lot of questionable ethics when we imagine the future of advanced robotics. If a robot is capable of being confused with a human, should we give robots the rights of humans such as a minimum wage? Should we develop an industry of robots that are specifically set to an AI level that is not capable of sentience so that we can still have non-citizenship robots? How far can a machine learning algorithm go before we can effectively say that if we go any further then the machine will gain the right to have citizenship? This is a very huge question when it comes to business because the more advanced we make our robots; the more jobs and skills can be performed by those robots. Therefore, all businesses looking into machine-learning need to keep this in mind if they plan on making machines capable of replacing workers.

Evil Intentions

Just because you build the most beneficial machine learning algorithm that exists doesn't mean that somebody won't try to make sure that you cannot share it with the world. As a business, we need to make sure that we develop security around the machine learning algorithms that are put in control of vital systems. Machine learning algorithms can handle what the human condition can't compensate for, but if we make machines capable of handling these vital systems then we also need to make sure that these machines can't be targeted. After all, we have seen over the years that no matter how beefy the security, there will always be a hole in it. Since we are making these machines of code, we need to make sure that the code that we write has as few holes as possible and has as many layers of protection as we can possibly build around them. Likewise, we need to pay very close attention to how much the machine learning algorithms have control, and whether there is an oversight of that control or not.

AI Control

This actually leads to our next topic as to whether we should allow AI to control certain aspects of our lives. It is a real possibility that the robots that we develop could gain the knowledge needed to recognize us as parasitic rather than beneficial to the survival of living creatures. There will come a time where humans are no longer able to comprehend the amount of complexity that's inside of a robot and whether we control that complex robot or not is essential in knowing whether the human race will still be alive x amount of years from now or not. An AI system could easily self-develop to replicate itself so that it could take out its creators because its creators can ensure that the robot is no longer living. So, if we create a machine learning algorithm that understands self-preservation, then we might have some trouble ahead of us. Needless to say, it's very important to gain a control on just how complex an AI can get.

Chapter 7: Machine Learning

You probably already have a pretty good idea of what machine learning is but maybe the explanations you've gotten are just a little bit cloudy. You know it's a key component of artificial intelligence but even that definition is a little fuzzy. It can be very difficult to wrap your head around the concept. It helps to understand that the foundation of Machine learning lies firmly rooted in our own biology.

For eons, we've viewed the human brain as the only creation with the ability to learn and process information from complex data. Now, we're told that inanimate objects can learn and change their behavior through this new innovation. It boggles the mind to think of it that way. However, there is a good reason why it is not only possible but is already a major part of how we live and do business today.

What is it?

To put it in the simplest of terms, machine learning is the art of computer programming that allows the computer to learn and to automatically adjust its functions to perfect how well they accomplish their task. A computer with machine learning capabilities can actually improve their performance based on their own experience without having an explicit program to tell them exactly what to do.

This process of learning actually begins with the ability of the program to observe collected data and compare it with previous data to find patterns and results and adjust itself accordingly. All of this is done through a complex system of neural networks and algorithms working together in order to produce the desired results. In essence, it means that computers are slowly beginning to learn to think like humans, learning from their experiences and changing in order to improve the results they pick up.

This is done in a wide variety of ways which we will discuss in later chapters of this book. It is now one of the most effective means of simplifying work that has to be done. By reducing the need for every program to be written for every possible function a machine can do, it allows the machine to teach itself how to perform the work done in a faster and more efficient manner.

If you're not quite sure how this works, let's use an example. Suppose you need to create a program that requires the computer to filter out certain types of data. In the traditional programming method, you would have to 1) have a human examine what data you want to be eliminated and then compile a list of ways that unwanted data might appear and identify the specific patterns that may appear. 2) Then the human would have to write a specific algorithm created to teach the computer exactly what to look for. 3) The human would then have to develop a software program that could identify those patterns and other details and label them accordingly. 4) Test the program and find any anomalies that could create a problem in finding the unwanted data and then go back to step one and repeat the process over and over again until the program is actually perfected.

Even with this pretty basic list of steps, you would only be able to program the computer to complete one task and would have to repeat the process for any other task that you also may need the computer to do. To complete all of these tasks, you will have to comply with an extensive list of rules in order for it to work correctly. This leaves your programming efforts open to errors popping up and disrupting the whole process. However, if you had chosen to use machine learning to accomplish the same thing, the process would have been done much more quickly with less risk of errors developing.

In addition, once the program is updated using the traditional method, the designer of the program could never feel like the job is done. He (or she) will always have to periodically go back and update it on a regular basis to ensure that it is compatible with the latest technology being used at the time. This would have to be done repeatedly until it is replaced by another program altogether.

Machine learning is a technique that once uploaded will run itself. It will automatically tell when updates need to be made and can even latch onto a system and get its own updates, freeing up the human to do other things. Machine learning makes it possible to solve even the most complex of problems with minimal human interference. Depending on the type of machine learning you use, once its live and active in the system, the machine can continue to make its own adjustments and recognize its own failures and successes for as long as it remains that way.

There are many advantages to using machine learning in computer programming today but no doubt there will be many more new ways to use it in the future. Right now, it is primarily used to...

• Solve problems that involve long lists of rules

• Solve very complex problems that do not have any apparent solution

• Adapt to new data in non-stable environments

As more and more people become aware of how great machine learning can be, it is likely that it will be used in hundreds or thousands of other purposes. In time, it is feasible that it will be used in every industry in existence and may be used at some point to even create new ones.

Types of Machine learning

There are several different types of machine learning that can be used right now, each used to accomplish a different type of problem and every day new approaches to it are being published.

When looking at different types of machine learning (ML) programs, they can all be categorized in two different ways; by form or function.

ML learning style programming can be either supervised or unsupervised and the form of function can be any type of classification, regression, decision tree, clustering, or deep learning type program. Regardless of the type used, all ML programming must contain the following:

• Representation: consisting of a group of classifiers or a basic language that the computer can understand

• Evaluation: a means of taking data and scoring it based on the program's objective

- Optimization: a strategy that gets you from the input data to the expected output

These three components are the basis for any learning algorithms that will be used to program the machine learning techniques into the computer. The primary goal of these algorithms is to help the computer to generalize and process data beyond its original programming so it can literally interpret new data that it may have never worked with before.

Machine learning types can also be categorized based on whether or not they have been "trained" by humans. Supervised and semi-supervised training requires some level of human interface in order to work effectively, but unsupervised and reinforcement learning can pretty much work entirely on their own without human interference.

Other factors that could categorize them could be:

- How they learn

- How simple or complex they are

The fact is that there is a lot to learn about machine learning. It is an extremely versatile program that can be applied in nearly every computer situation there is. However, before you can determine exactly which type of machine learning you will need, you'll have to first take a very close look at the problem you are facing and make your decisions from there.

It is true that deep learning has accomplished many things since it was first introduced. Because of its versatility and adaptability in so many situations, it has enabled computers to be able to detect speech patterns, create text-to-speech programs, retrieve information when needed, and even predict consumer usage in different industries. We have become more dependent on these programs than we may realize, and we are sure to see more of this cutting edge type of programming in the very near future in the field of healthcare, robotics, marketing, and more.

Supervised vs. Unsupervised Learning

A machine learning system can be labeled accordingly based on how much human interaction it needs to function. There are many different classifications for this but there are four primary categories you may see when studying machine learning basics: supervised, unsupervised, semi-supervised, and reinforcement learning. These labels are simply descriptions of the different ways that algorithms make it possible for machines to perform functions, make decisions, and analyze data. With each of these, the machine is expected to learn something from each task it performs. Let's begin by taking a closer look at what these categories actually are and how they work.

1)Supervised Learning

• In supervised learning, the machine is already programmed to expect a certain output of an algorithm in its system before it begins its work. In essence, it knows the kind of answer it is trying to reach, and simply needs to work out the different steps needed to find it. The algorithm is learned by a specialized set of training data that "guides" the machine to the right conclusion. So, if something goes wrong and the algorithms produce a result that is vastly different from the expected outcome, the training data previously entered will step in and redirect the functions so that the computer gets back on track.

• The majority of machine learning is supervised learning where the input variable (x) is the primary tool that is manipulated to reach the output variable (y) by using the different algorithms. All of this data - the input variable, the expected output, and the algorithm is provided by humans.

• Supervised learning can be categorized further into two different ways: classification and regression.

• When working with classification problems, all the variables are grouped together based on the output. This type of programming can be used in analyzing demographic data, i.e. marital status, sex, or age. So, if you are given a large number of images, each with its own set of identifying data, you could program the computer to analyze those images and acquire enough information to recognize and identify new images in the future.

• Regression works on problems that include situations where the output variables are set as real numbers. In this case, you could have a large number of molecules with varying combinations to make up different drugs. With supervised training, you could program the computer to analyze the data and then use it to determine if new molecules introduced into the system make up drugs or some other type of matter.

• There are many practical applications for classification and regression with supervised learning. Some algorithms can also be used for both but we'll discuss that in more detail later on.

• Some of the most commonly used algorithms in supervised learning include:

• K-nears neighbors

• Linear regression

• Neural networks

• Support vector machines

• Logistic regression

• Decision trees and random forests

2)Unsupervised Learning

• Unsupervised learning is not as common as supervised learning but it is probably the most important aspect of machine learning that you will need. It is this type of learning will be the key to the effectiveness of artificial intelligence and other similar developments in the future. The basic concept behind unsupervised learning is to have the machine teach itself without human interference.

• With unsupervised learning, the system is not provided with any preexisting data and the outcomes of the problems are not already known. In other words, the program is working blind using only logical operations to chart its path to a decision. This makes problem solving under unsupervised learning very challenging, but it is this type of learning that is more closely linked to the way the human mind processes information.

• It is more often used as a means of predicting, interpreting, or finding solutions to an unlisted amount of data by taking the input data and analyzing it against the basic binary logo mechanism already included in every computer system.

• Unlike supervised learning, where data is fed into the system, the unsupervised learning model allows you to submit data for analysis with no previous existing information to base decisions on. For example, if you were to input an image with several different geometric shapes in it, the system would analyze the image to learn as much as possible from it. It works on its own to identify the problem, classify what information it has, and then classify that information based on the different shapes, sizes, and colors and then labels it accordingly.

• Inevitably there will be wrong answers but with each wrong answer, it will go back and reanalyze the data and make the necessary adjustments. With each attempt to solve a problem, the degree of probability will be reduced.

• The value of unsupervised learning, however, lies in the machine's ability to recognize when it has made a mistake and how it adjusts its analysis to correct it.

• Some of the most commonly used algorithms in unsupervised learning include:

• Clustering; K-means, hierarchical cluster analysis

• Association rule learning: Eclat, priori

• Visualization and dimensionality reduction

3)Semi-Supervised Learning

Semi-supervised learning is merely a hybrid combination of both supervised and unsupervised. To understand it better, it helps to first understand the difference between the first two. With supervised learning, the algorithms are designed and trained based on datasets that have already been labeled by a human engineer. This data is used to guide the machine to the right conclusion. With unsupervised learning, the algorithms are not given any prelabeled data, so the system must analyze the data and determine what is important to them and draw its own conclusions. With semi-supervised learning, this difference is minimized, as the system is provided with a combination of both labeled data and unlabeled.

There are many reasons why one might choose this method. First, it is not always practical to label all the data that is needed for computer programming. Labeling millions of pictures is not only time consuming, it can also be extremely cost-prohibitive. In addition, complete interference by humans can run the risk of creating biases on the computer model. To balance this out, offering a modest collection of labeled data during the training process and testing with unlabeled data seems to produce more effective and accurate results.

In many cases, it is the preferred option for situations like webpage classification, speech recognition, and for other extremely complex analysis like genetic sequencing. It allows you to access massive volumes of unlabeled data where the process of identifying and assigning labels would represent an insurmountable task.

4)Reinforcement Learning

This style of machine learning is very similar to what happens in a psychiatrist's office. The basic concept here is very similar to unsupervised learning in that it allows a great deal of control to be given to the software and the machines to determine what the appropriate action should be. Here, feedback is necessary in order to let the machine know if it is making progress or not so it can adapt its behavior accordingly.

The algorithms used here help the machines learn based on the outcome of the decisions they make. It is a complex system that relies on a large number of different algorithms working together to determine what happens next to achieve the desired results or to solve a specific problem.

When compared to other types of machine learning, the differences are made very clear. In supervised learning, there is a human supervisor who has the knowledge of the current environment and shares that knowledge in the form of data to help the machine to understand the problem and come up with the solution. However, there may be many subtasks that the system can perform without that human interaction. So, there are times when the computer can learn from its own experiences.

In both supervised and reinforcement learning, there is a function called computer mapping happening between the input data and the output data. But with reinforcement learning, there is an additional "reward" function that gives the system enough feedback so that it can gauge its progress and redirect its path when needed.

This same mapping function also exists in unsupervised learning. However, with unsupervised learning, the reward system does not exist. The primary focus of the machine is to locate patterns and identify properties rather than measuring progress toward an actual end goal. For example, if the machine is tasked to recommend a news report for the user, with reinforcement learning, the system will examine past feedback from the user and then create a graph of news reports that are in line with their past personal interests. But with unsupervised learning, it will look at past history and try to identify a pattern and select a report that matches with that particular pattern.

There are other types of machine learning that may not be as common or well recognized. These include batch learning, where the system is given all the data at one time, not in smaller increments; online learning where the system processes data in small increments or in small groups; instance-based learning, which is predominantly a simple memorization program; model-based learning where the system learns from examples and then is asked to make predictions.

It is important to understand that while machines can effectively learn, they are not like little tiny humans who already know how to tell the difference between a pineapple and an orange, or those that can, without much input, determine colors, shapes, sizes, etc. In order for machines to learn, they must have a great deal of quality data input even for the simplest of programs in order for them to be effective.

This means that a great deal of care must be taken when choosing the type of data you use to program the computer. If your data is not relevant, accurate, and reliable it will be full of errors that will make it very difficult for the machine to do its job. So, the key here is to make sure that you're giving it quality data and basing your algorithms on that data.

Chapter 8: Neural Networks

Those not directly involved in machine learning, the average Joe, would probably be very surprised to learn that they have already interacted with plenty of artificial intelligence and other forms of machine learning. Global leaders like Amazon, Apple, Facebook, Google, and IBM have spent millions of dollars on research and applications that will take their businesses to the next level.

Some of that research is already impacting us on a daily basis without us even knowing about it. A good example of this is every time you do a search on the internet, as soon as you insert a keyword into the search box, it is machine learning that scans the millions of websites and compiles a list of those sites that closely fit your search criteria.

You also see evidence of it in spam filters for your email, or on Netflix when it recommends the next shows for you to watch. It's used in the medical industry to classify medications, and it's a huge part of the Human Genome Project as it sifts through the billions of combinations of DNA patterns that may relate some hidden secret about your family history, health prospects, and risk factors.

These systems are highly sophisticated and can be adapted to every other industry that exists around us. All of them are made possible by the use of algorithms that are designed to guide the computer through various learning processes. With the right algorithm, a system can identify abnormal behavior that goes against a set pattern and teach itself to predict possible outcomes for a wide variety of situations.

These algorithms, data receptors and everything else that make all of this possible are contained within something called an artificial neural network. Since they were first introduced in the 1950's, they have been seen as a panacea for the future of science. Patterned after the human brain, their main role is to allow a machine to learn while in the training phase of programming and then use that knowledge to apply to future situations.

What are They and How They Work?

When you think of terms like deep learning, artificial intelligence, and machine learning it all refers to what is happening to the neural network. When we say the machine learns, it really means that the neural networks are being trained in the same way as the human brain.

A good way to think of these networks is to think of many simple parallel processors integrated with hundreds (or thousands) of tiny connections that make up a computational distributed model. In the human brain, there are millions of neurons all interconnected by synapses that allow them to make computations and analysis in the cerebral cortex. As these connections are made, learning is achieved allowing the person to acquire new skills so they can accomplish complex problems.

In neural networks, however, there are hundreds of homogeneous processing units that are interconnected through links. The beauty of the design is in its simplicity and in the unique configuration of the connections. The data is entered through designated input units and travels through several layers of units as it computes the problem until it reaches the output layer, which communicates a final decision that is to be carried out by the program.

In its earliest days, the structure of a neural network was extremely simple with only a few units to transmit information. Today though, a single network could conceivably have millions of units all intertwined and working together to recreate the learning process. The more modern networks are capable of solving extremely complex problems in a wide variety of areas.

The McCulloch-Pitt's Neuron - What is It?

We now understand that a neural network is a computer system that has been designed to mimic the way the human brain works. In fact, there are a lot of similarities between the human brain and an artificial neural network:

• They are formed by millions of artificial neurons, each able to compute and come up with a solution

• Each neuron (unit) has many weighted connections

• They are parallel and non-linear

• They are trainable - learning happens when the connections' weight changes

• They do not penalize the system for errors but can actually adapt to new knowledge

• They can produce outputs based on new input data they have never encountered before

On the surface, they work very similarly to the human brain but let's take a little time to look at how a single unit works. While all of the above describes how the entire neural network actually functions, the McCulloch-Pitt's neuron is the smallest part of a network.

In the human brain, a neuron is the smallest unit of mental processing there is. In an artificial neural network (ANN), this unit (the neuron) is the fundamental means of performing any type of calculation. It is comprised of three basic elements.

• The connections, characterized by weight or synaptic efficacy

• A summing agent that processes the input signals and their synapses to come up with a sum of linear combinations

• An activation function that limits the extent of the neuron's output

The McCulloch-Pitts (MCP) neuron was introduced in the early 1940s and was named after neuroscientist Warren S. McCulloch, and the logician Walter Pitts. Their goal was to try to understand exactly what happened in the human brain to produce the complex patterns and then mimic them by connecting many basic cells together.

In their original design, there were many limitations that prevented the machine from actually "learning." The design was very simple - the inputs were limited to either a zero or a one and the output was also limited to a zero or a one. Every input was either excitatory or inhibitory.

The function of the MCP neuron was, to sum up all the inputs. So, if an input value was one and it was excitatory (positive), another one was added. If it was one and inhibitory (negative), then a one was subtracted from the sum. This process was done for every input and then a total sum was determined.

If the result was less that a preset value, then the output would be zero, if it was more, then the output would be one.

As you can see from the image, the data is represented with different variables. The variables W1, W2, and W3, show which of the inputs are actually excitatory and which ones are inhibitory. If the subscript number is a positive one then that is an excitatory weight and if the number is a negative one it is an inhibitory weight.

The inputs are represented by the X weights at the beginning of the neuron (X1, X2, X3). There are no limits to the number of inputs that could be included in the MCP neuron so the final sum of all the weights could vary widely from one situation to the next. However, if you think about it, it is possible to calculate the sum using the x's and the w's similar to the problem below.

Sum = X1W1 + X2W2 + X3W3 and so on.

This type of equation is referred to as the "weighted sum."

When that sum is calculated, you can then check if the sum is < or > than T. If it is less than T, the output would be a zero, if it is more than T, the output would be 1. While this was a pretty basic concept, it wasn't long before people began to discover they could accomplish many amazing things with it as can be seen from the following examples.

In the above example, you see what is called a NOR gate, which gives you an output of 1 because all the inputs are zero (X1, X2, X3). You could experiment with different end case scenarios by varying the input from either zero or one.

In the above example, you have two neurons. The first neurons are the receivers and will accept the inputs you provide and the second is dedicated to working on the output of the first neuron. It is not involved nor does it have any access to any of the initial input data.

In the above example, you can see how a 3-input is created using the MCP neuron. A NAND gate will only give a zero if all the inputs are 1. The neuron in this figure needs 4 neurons. It takes the output of the first three inputs and uses it to create the input of the fourth.

The MCP neuron was extremely basic in its design but very effective in its approach. The MCP neuron is no longer in use today. This is mainly because the NOR and NAND gates already have extremely efficient circuitry so it was no longer necessary to use them in less efficient models. The goal was to use the interconnections in the best possible way.

Today, we have access to much more advanced neurons where the inputs can have even more practical uses. Now both neurons and their weights can have decimal values.

The model also had a threshold value that could influence the resulting effects based on whether it was positive or negative. In basic mathematical terms, this could be described as a "K" neuron which can be used in equations so they can actually process and calculate the sums, rather than just doing a check to see if it is less than or greater than the predetermined figure.

Neural Network Architecture

Within the neural network architecture, there are three basic types of activation functions at work. Threshold functions, which were commonly used in the McCulloch-Pitts neuron model, the Piecewise-linear functions, and the Sigmoid functions, which are more commonly used in the development of today's artificial neural networks. Neural Network Architecture gives a perfect balance between the linear and the non-linear behaviors as you can see in the example below:

You can see here that the α is the parameter that shows the actual slope of the function.

The actual structure of the network architecture depends on which algorithm you are using. There are three separate classes of networks that can be used.

• One Layer Feedforward Networks: This is a very basic type of layered network. There are input knots and an output layer of neurons involved. The signal moves through the network starting at the input layer and moving linearly until it reaches the output layer. None of the connections will move back again through the system and there are no transversal connections that cut across any other connection in the output layer.

• Multilayer Feedforward Networks: These networks are slightly different in that they have one or more hidden layers that lie in between the input and the output layers. Each of these layers has connections that can receive incoming data from the previous layer and other connections that send output data to the next one. This way, a signal propagation happens in a linear fashion without the need of cycles or transverse connections. With this type of network, there is an increase in interactions between the different neurons giving it a broader and more global perspective.

• Recurring Networks: These networks function on a cyclical basis. The use of cycles can have a major effect on how a machine learns and on how it performs. The result is a much more dynamic system.

The process of machine learning is made possible by giving set parameters to a neural network and giving it the ability to adapt to various types of stimulation from its surrounding environment. This type of learning happens by the way the machine adapts to this stimulation.

Adaptations happen when a set of rules (or parameters) are given based on what is called a "learning algorithm." There are two fundamental kinds of learning algorithms that we have already discussed; supervised and unsupervised. Using these algorithms there are several different ways the machine can actually learn:

• Error Correction: When a neuron receives an input and generates a response, the machine knows what the desired response should be. If the machine makes a mistake it is given an error signal that will activate a control mechanism that will initiate a series of adjustments in the neuron so that the next response will be closer to the desired answer. In this method of learning, the machine will continue to process the data this way until it can produce the expected response.

• Memory-Based Learning: In this case, the machine stores all of its past experiences in its memory. Any correctly classified data is preserved and can be accessed. When a classification of data is needed on an experience the machine has never before encountered, it will access its data banks searching for related examples to process the new information. This type of learning is based on two fundamental factors: the basic ingredients and the criteria needed to define the test vector.

• One example of this type of learning style is what is called the "nearest neighbor method" where the machine selects from its memory an example that is closest to the test subject.

• There is also the k-nearest neighbor method where the neighborhood of the sample is not one but instead the set of k examples that are stored close together. With this method, the assigned class is based on the one that has the highest frequency surrounding the sample.

• Hebbian Learning: This method is based on the point when the A neuron's axon or its output transmission line is close enough to be excitable to neuron B. This will repeatedly and persistently cause an action potential triggering a growth process in one or sometimes even both neurons that will increase the efficacy of neuron A. All of this is based on two different rules:

• If both neurons are connected by a synapse and are activated at the same time, then the weight associated with the synapse will progressively increase.

• If both neurons are not activated at the same time then the weight of the synapse is progressively decreased and, in some cases, completely eliminated.

• This type of synapse is referred to as a Hebbian synapse. Based on the above rules when the correlation of the signals causes an increase in synapse efficacy, it can be referred to as a Hebbian modification. However, if it causes a reduction then it can be referred to as an anti-Hebbian.

• Competitive Learning: In competitive learning, the neurons are actually in competition with one another in an attempt to become active. Each neuron can only be active at a certain point in time. Competitive learning is comprised of three basic elements.

• The neurons must all be identical. However, if there is a set of randomly generated synaptic weights, they will respond in a different way to the set of inputs provided.

• There must be a limit to each neuron's strength

• There has to be a mechanism in place that makes it possible for the neurons to compete for the chance to respond to the preset of inputs so that only one will be active at any given time.

• The winner-takes-all neuron is the one that wins that right

• By using the neurons in a way that allows the user to specialize and tailor a set of similar inputs the machine can start to recognize set features of various classes of inputs. In its most basic form, the neural network would have only one layer of input neurons and one layer of output neurons, all connected together by input knots or synapses or forward excitatory connections. In more complex systems there may also be lateral inhibitions and inhibitory feedback connections at work as well.

Training the Neural network

When it comes to training a neural network, there are several different methods that have proven to be very effective. However, there is one method that seems to have the most positive results. The error propagation algorithm sometimes referred to as the error backpropagation. This method systematically adjusts the weight of all the different connections of the neurons. In this way, the responses can gradually get closer and closer to the preferred end result.

There are two stages to this type of training: the forward propagation, which is stage 1, and the back propagation or stage 2.

In stage 1, all the activated neurons from the very first layer all the way to the final layer are calculated. In this stage, the weight of the synaptic connections remains fixed. This means that with the first iteration the system will only use the default values. However, during stage 2, the actual answer from the network, the actual output will be compared to the expected output so that the actual error rate can be determined.

The resulting error rate is then propagated and reversed back to one of the synaptic connections where the weights are modified in an attempt to reduce the difference between the result and the expected output. The process is repeated until the error rate cannot be reduced any further.

• Forward Propagation: with forward propagation, input X enters the initial data that is then spread to the hidden layers of the system until it finally produces an output. The basic architecture of the network determines every aspect of this data including its depth, width, and activation functions. The depth shows how many hidden layers there are, the width shows how many units on each layer and the activation functions tell the system exactly what to do.

• Backward Propagation: utilizes a supervised learning algorithm that allows the weight of the connections to be adjusted with the sole purpose of reducing the difference in value between the current solution to a problem and the expected solution.

There are many advantages to training neural networks and utilizing them in machine learning. It is a highly innovative field of study and has a great deal of potential in the future of computer science.

• They are capable of solving problems that require answers that result in a degree of error

• They can generalize and produce answers to problems that they have not been trained for

• They can be easily implemented by defining a neuron, duplicating, and creating the associated connections

• They can compute operations quickly because every neuron uses only the value it receives as input

• They can produce stable outputs related to the input values

• They can evaluate all inputs at the same time to produce a result

Still, even with all those advantages, neural networks do have a few drawbacks that can make things more complicated.

• Its function can be similar to that of a black box; you can't go back and understand why it produced the result it created. You can only determine what happened.

• The memory cannot be localized within the network nor can it be described

• Because of their unique computer needs, they can only be used on those computers that have compatible hardware

• They do require extensive training techniques that can use up an extensive amount of time to produce the proper calculations

• They can only solve problems if they have been given the right algorithm to do it

• The output values can vary in their accuracy

• They require a large number of examples in order to create a good learning process to produce the right solution.

Neural networks are completely capable of independent decision making based on the number of inputs and variables. Because of this, they are able to create an unlimited number of recurring iterations to solve problems without human interference. When we see these networks in action, you'll find a numeric vector that represents the various types of input data. These vectors could be anything from pixels, audio and/or video signals, or just plain words. These vectors can be adjusted via a series of functions producing an output result.

Clearly, there is much more involved in neural networks than meets the eye. They can handle very basic problems and more complex problems using the same system.

The only difference is the number of weights that are applied to the input values.

Chapter 9: How It All Relates To Deep Learning

All this technical information can be very exciting for the right person. We've entertained the thought of machine learning since the early days of science fiction. The idea of creating a machine that can learn enough to adapt its behavior is utterly fascinating. Still, it is important to get a full grasp of deep learning and its various applications we can already use in real life.

We know a neural network is designed to give you the same response when the same input values are entered. It has no memory to speak of but when the input has been given, it will react the same way to it every time. We call this behavior a stateless algorithm.

In most instances, this is all we need for a computer to function. However, it has its limitations. What happens when data is entered that has some variations in value and is not the same? For example, if you were asked to predict something that was about to happen, how would you go about it? You might access your previous memories and experiences stored in your mind to gauge the probability of certain events repeating themselves. You may not be able to guess with one hundred percent accuracy, but you could narrow down your options to several logical choices.

However, what happens when you are expected to guess events at random with only a few events that are precursors to the event you want to predict? In such a case, you would analyze the events prior to the expected event and determine the probability of what would happen next. In the human brain, it is pretty easy to determine possibilities when we know the sequence of events that came before. There are many clouds in the sky, with each passing hour the clouds are getting darker and darker. The temperature begins to drop, and the wind begins to increase in intensity. The logical probability here is that a storm is approaching.

With a neural network in deep learning, before this can happen memory must be added to the system. Anytime you need a response from the program, you will have to save a series of calculations that can be reused as input each time this problem comes up. So, with each problem solved, the computer will grow in its experience and knowledge so that it can adapt its predictions based on a growing body of knowledge.

This basic concept is referred to as a recurrent neural network, where the system actually goes through an upgrade each time it is used. This makes it possible for predictions and responses to vary based on new data and experiences. Over time, this can lead to the system recognizing patterns and other variables as long as the memory supports it.

We see this kind of application working in machines we interact with every day. A perfect example of this is your smart phone. When you are sending a text message you are automatically given a series of options to suggest the next word you might want to write. When you surf the internet, you are often given suggestions and advertisements based on past websites you've visited. We are often given recommendations for things to buy, movies to watch, foods to eat, and even places to go. All these things are the result of this kind of predictive algorithms that are used in deep learning.

The only difference is that eventually, predictions will be more extensive and not simply a word or a suggestion. With deep learning, it can one day be possible for entire stories to be written using neural networks. Eventually, recurrent neural networks will be able to match the style and practices of human brains in a vast number of ways.

How Does it Work

As we have already seen, learning happens when a machine makes a wrong prediction and must adjust its variables to minimize the percentage of error. Without some type of feedback that lets the machine know its error rate, this type of adaptation is impossible. There must be a way for the error to be fed back into the system, analyzed, and understood in order for the corrections to be made.

When a neural network is first initiated, the values of the different arrays and their weights are usually randomly assigned and adjusted as the machine receives its error feedback. This highlights the true purpose of the neural network: to rearrange after each iteration, the values of the weights in order to create a prediction that is closer to the expected output.

While this may seem logical and simple when it comes to the human mind that is naturally designed to do this in a fraction of a second, getting a machine to do it is not all that easy. The process of training an ANN to learn can be quite complex, especially when it comes to areas like speech recognition, self-driving cars, or computer vision. For this, you not only need all of the parts working as they should, but you will also need to generate a great deal of computational power and speed.

In recent years, this has been made possible by the use of graphics cards, which have allowed for new results to be used in parallel in order to speed up the process of computer predictions.

For a neural network to perform properly it must have quality raw data that can be extracted from the input. This data must be analyzed and packaged so that the machine is able to pull out any properties that could be of use in the learning process.

In the past, it required humans to manually identify these properties and input them into the machine. Basically, if the data was known it was fed into the neural network, then stored in its memory. This method of manually feeding data to the machine took up a lot of man hours to do. When the system received data that had already been received and analyzed before, it would recognize the similarities and store it as a past experience. So, by providing a wider variety of inputs, the machine could become more flexible in adapting information.

With deep learning, there is no longer a need for this type of human interaction, as the machine now has the capability of picking up the necessary raw data completely on its own. As more and more data is accumulated, the machine's ability to think and to learn improves.

The term "deep" is not to mean that the computer is in deep thought like a human, but it refers to the various levels of data received over time, each time allowing the system to learn and improve its performance, adding more depth of knowledge and experience. As this depth increases, the goal is to eventually develop the type of networks that can be 100% independent of human interaction.

Deep learning is a relatively new aspect of machine learning. This is because up until very recently, the kind of processing power and storage capabilities available were not sufficient enough to allow this type of learning to happen. However, now that it does exist and is readily available, this type of machine learning is becoming a new foundation of an entirely new form of technology.

As a result, deep learning has become the base foundation of all sorts of highly progressive artificial intelligence and can be applied in all types of areas. Already it is being used in speech recognition programs, image recognition, and self-driving cars. It is being applied in advanced robotics and has already been introduced in the medical imaging field as a means of making more accurate and reliable diagnoses of patients. It is used to operate drones, maintain other machines, and a host of other applications.

As a practical example of machine learning, let's take a look at how this ability can make a major change in one professional field. The primary role of a radiologist is to analyze thousands of radiographic images and make medical determinations. His expert eye is quickly able to spot anomalies such as a tumor or another foreign body that could be impacting a patient's health. If he makes a mistake, it could have severe consequences that could amount to life or death.

However, with deep learning software, the machine can examine millions of the same radiographic images and store them in its memory, never forgetting a single one. Its ability to analyze an image and extract similarities from the millions of similar images will allow it to give a much more accurate diagnosis of a patient's medical condition.

The same software could be adapted to other industries as well. The fact is that deep learning has the potential to change the world as we know it. We already rely on a GPS system to tell us how to get to a destination we have never been before. It is not a huge leap to having vehicles drive themselves. Machines can already analyze traffic conditions, signs, speed limits, obstacles and so on. The next evolution will be much, much more efficient than the clunky GPS systems we're using today.

Main Architecture

This area of machine learning is characterized by a system that works on more than one layer. Each layer is capable of receiving input from the one before it. With input received on each layer, the data is transformed, giving more insight to the machine. Therefore, the machine doesn't just learn with each problem it gives, but it learns on each layer of data as it passes through the system.

You might liken each layer to the different areas found in the human brain's cerebral cortex. The visual cortex, as an example, is responsible for not just seeing objects but has the ability to recognize them. This is the part of the brain that can identify images, recognize sequences, etc. In our brains, each of the sections has a very specific hierarchal order.

When our brain receives an image, it doesn't just immediately label it, but it processes it through several different stages. First, it must detect the edges, then it perceives the shape, and then it deciphers the colors, etc. Of course, all of this happens at the lightning speed of 13 milliseconds; if you're watching a movie it is about the speed of 75 frames a second. Neural networks, infused with deep learning, have a very similar hierarchal order. Even a simple network of three layers is now capable of distinguishing things in all kinds of environments and situations.

As data passes through the different layers it can select different aspects of the data and disregard those details that do not apply to the problem it is working on. There are several different types of deep learning networks:

• Discriminatory Feedforward Models: used to classify data

• Unsupervised Training: used to reconstruct the input and pre-train other models

• Recurring Models: used for sequencing, speech recognition, sentiment analysis, etc.

• Reinforcement Learning: used for machines that need to learn and mimic behaviors

It is clear that the algorithms and techniques used in deep learning make it possible for machines to find patterns, analyze situations, and identify regularities and irregularities in a wide range of areas. By doing so, it can actually help cut costs as it will no longer require input to be provided by humans. With so many thousands of input data becoming a part of this type of software, it is now possible that the computer has learned enough to automatically extract the data it needs entirely on its own. There's no telling what we will be able to expect in the future when it comes to the capabilities of a deep learning network.

Chapter 4: Algorithms

At its most basic level, machine learning is the use of different preprogrammed algorithms that collect and analyze data in order to determine possible outcomes within an acceptable range. Each time these algorithms receive new data the system learns and adapts to improve performance.

We've already touched on some of the most commonly used categories of algorithms: supervised, semi-supervised, unsupervised, and reinforcement, but now we're going to take a closer look at what an algorithm actually is, and some of the more popular types that can be used in machine learning.

Basically, an algorithm is a sequence of steps that will allow a machine to accomplish a specific task. It is important to point out here that while we refer to computers as using algorithms, they are not just limited to these types of machines. Other devices can also make use of algorithms as well.

There are three core characteristics that are contained in all algorithms:

• They must be finite: it has to have an end

• It has to have clear instructions

• It must be effective

Algorithms are mathematical entities, and while they are so much a part of modern technology, it is difficult to believe that they have already been in use for thousands of years. Archaeologists and historians have discovered records of them dating as far back as 1600 BC. These mathematical formulas can be applied in a wide range of settings.

Commonly Used Algorithms You Should Know

While there are hundreds of algorithms that can be used in machine learning, this chapter is going to focus only on those needed for computing software. Below we have some of the most commonly used algorithms, their purpose, and how they can be applied.

Linear Regression

Linear regression is probably the most well-known of all the algorithms associated with machine learning. The fundamental concept of this algorithm is to find the path that best models the linear trend, or in other words, finding the line that best fits the problem. It assumes that a linear relationship exists between the different input variables.

When there is only one input variable (x), the method used is called a simple linear regression but if there are multiple input variables, the method is referred to as multiple linear regression.

The very nature of a linear algorithm is to combine a specified group of input variables where the solution is an actual predicted output. In such cases, both input and output values have to be numeric in nature.

Each input value is given a single scale factor called a coefficient. It can be identified by the capital Greek letter Beta (B). Another coefficient is added so the line has another degree of freedom allowing it to move up or down along a two-dimensional plot line. This is referred to as the bias coefficient.

Y + B0 +B1*X

When there are higher dimensions and you're working with additional inputs it is referred to as a hyper-plane.

If a coefficient is zero it cancels out the effect of the input variable. This type of scenario is relevant in conditions where you need a means of regulating the changes and adaptations within the neural network. There are several ways linear regression can be applied.

• Simple Linear Regression can be used when you have single input variable used to estimate coefficients. It allows you to calculate statistical properties extracted from the input data like means, deviations, correlations, and covariance.

• Ordinary Least Squares are used when you have more than one input and you need to estimate the values of the coefficients. It treats the data as a matrix and applies linear algebraic operations to perform the estimations.

• Gradient Descent is used when you have multiple inputs to process the values of the coefficients. It works by using random values for every coefficient. The sum of the errors is then calculated for the input and output values to determine a learning rate. This is then used as a scale that can help to update the results in an effort to reduce the rate of error.

• Finally, there is regularization. These are extensions created to minimize the rate of error during the training phase, but they are also used to simplify the complexity of the model.

Logistic Regression

Logistic regression is very popular when you need to resolve binary classification problems. This is when the solution can be one of only two options. Sometimes referred to as dichotomy, it works well with problems that require either a true/false or yes/no answer.

To understand logistic regression better, you first have to have a clear understanding of linear regression. As an analyst, you must find the best line to show a specific trend. This requires finding an equation that gives the best direct feature that addresses the regression problem.

The standard practice is to use the least square method, where the idea is to shorten the distance between the line and the training data. Basically, the system is looking for a line that is "nearest" to all the input data.

Logistic regression is a part of a specific type of algorithm called the generalized linear model. Unlike with linear regression, your objective is to find a model that comes closest to the final value of the outcome or the variable. However, remember that you are solving a binary problem so there is no set value to predict. It is just a matter of two possible outcomes. You're actually looking for the higher probability that one outcome will actually occur.

Problems that linear regression would solve: How many inches of snowfall will we get this year?

Problems that logical regression would solve: Will it snow tomorrow?

Decision Trees

Decision tree algorithms are more often used to classify a model and label it in a tree structure. Many analysts find them to be excellent tools that can give them accurate and reliable output data.

Decision trees are easy to read and understand. In fact, when using them you will be able to see exactly why you need certain classifiers in order to make a decision. If you are new to writing code this is probably the best algorithm to cut your teeth on.

These algorithms all have exactly the same approach; to breakdown the data into the smallest possible subsets (those that contain only one group of outcomes). The data is divided up based on whatever predictors are available. Then they group all subsets of the same class together. They will continue to do this until they have the smallest set of data possible.

Once this is accomplished, it is very easy to make a prediction as to the expected behavior. Making this type of prediction is very simple. All the system does is follow the path that matches the given predictors. It will lead to the subset that contains all the yes answers.

Support Vector Machines

Support Vector Machines or SVM, are algorithms that can be used like weapons. Unlike the others mentioned, SVMs can come up with solutions that are far more precise than any of the others we've talked about.

This type of algorithm is extremely complex and utilizes some of the most challenging mathematical equations there are. Because of this unique complexity, SVMs can only slice through very small amounts of datasets. So, if the initial training data is too extensive, it is likely that SVM is not the best option.

SVMs are used for classifications. It searches for the optimum dividing line between all the different classes of data the system may be considering. In short, it looks for the widest separation (or margin) of data that exists between all the many groupings or subsets available.

Naive Bayes

The Naive Bayes algorithm uses statistical modeling to perform classification problems. It is relatively simple, but it can provide very precise solutions when used in the right way. It is very scalable when compared to the support vector machines, probably the most complex of all the algorithms in use today.

Naive Bayes is based on the Bayes' Theorem that assumes that "all predictors are independent of each other."

This algorithm does not store any data in its memory, but it does study and analyze the training data and uses that knowledge to adapt accordingly.

In real life, all predictors are interdependent but with Naive Bayes, they are all viewed as separate and distinct from each other (naive). As the system analyzes the data, it assigns a probability to each of the predictors associating them each with a specific class that is independent of any other features. This is referred to as the "class-predictor probability.

As an example, consider how it would analyze and determine the class of a specific fruit. It might first analyze and determine that the fruit is red. The algorithm then taps into its knowledge of fruits and determines that there are red apples, cherries, and strawberries.

When it looks at the next classification, shape, it determines that the shape is round. Apples, oranges, and peaches are all round, but strawberries are not. Finally, it will look at the size in diameter. In this prediction, the fruit is 3" in diameter. This could now be an apple, an orange, a peach, or a pomegranate. Once all of the different characteristics are considered, it will assign a percentage of probability that the fruit is from several classes with the one with the highest percentage being the one most likely to fit the set parameters. It could look something like this:

Probability of Apple80%

Probability of Orange10%

Probability of Strawberry 5%

...and so on.

If you have studied algorithms before, one of the first things you learn is that there are hundreds and perhaps thousands of them. Machines can learn based on the algorithm you use. With the right algorithm, machine learning is not only likely but extremely possible.

Chapter 10: Machine Learning Applications

For anyone new to machine learning, the phrase "artificial intelligence" is probably the first term you can identify with. Believe it or not, it is not a thing of the future but already exists right now, today in many areas of life. This is because there are countless applications that can take advantage of this amazing type of programming in everyday life.

Right now, many of us are already using applications like Apple's Siri, Amazon's Alexa, and Google's NOW. These serve as virtual personal assistants that will listen to your commands and execute the required behavior on their own. They help you to find information, remember past requests, and send out commands to other devices to perform certain actions.

Most virtual assistants are voice-activated and can recognize and understand exactly what you say without the need for you to key in the information to activate it.

They can also make predictions when you're commuting. They can gather traffic data, use GPS navigation, and check on accident reports. The information is then used to create a real time picture of your route to your destination complete with detours around heavy traffic sites or construction zones.

You might also see them used in video surveillance for security jobs; they are frequently utilized in social media, email filtering, customer support, refining online data searches, making product recommendations, and even in fraud detection.

There are many ways machine learning has not only been helpful but has made it possible for many more things to be done that weren't possible only a few years ago.

Machine learning and "The Cloud"

You can even see it appearing in "the Cloud," which is the primary home base for many different applications. In the past, this was far out of reach for most people and businesses that didn't have the finances to store this much computing data in their own network of computers, nor did they have the technical knowledge required to design the necessary models to use.

Today, however, sites like Google, AWS, and Microsoft offer many options for storing machine learning data in the cloud where it can now be accessible from wherever you are in the world as long as you have an Internet connection.

These companies also provide SDKs or software developer kits that allow a user to actually embed the function directly into their needed applications, and most support all programming languages. Today, you don't need to know all the technical programming languages or have a computer science degree to take advantage of the many things that machine learning can do. You can actually use them from within whatever application you're using, completely unaware that you are interacting with a learning machine.

There are drawbacks though. As advanced as this new technology may be, it has yet to be perfected. For example, if you're accessing a machine learning application in the cloud, it is pretty much limited to that cloud. This means that if your database is not stored, or you have access to the cloud that the application is in, it is virtually useless to you.

So, if you, the user, choose to use one cloud provider, you will probably also have to use that same provider for all your data storage in order to take advantage of the applications it provides. But if there is an application stored on another provider's server, you may not be able to use it to your advantage.

There is no question that machine learning has made major strides in our modern day. While it does have limitations, its capabilities far outweigh those limitations on many fronts. As more and more people become aware of machine learning and what it can do, it will become a real game changer for everyone on the planet in some form or fashion.

Hybrid Applications

When it comes to artificial intelligence, machine learning applications really start to excel. Applications in general, are designed to give devices a wide bit of diversity that otherwise would not be possible. But with AI, the capabilities are even more advanced.

This is possible with the use of hybrid applications. While this field is very limited in the here and now, the future holds a lot of promise in the coming years. What can we expect from hybrid applications? A good way to answer that is by comparing two AI-driven technologies that are already in use today: the IBM Watson and the Tesla Model S.

These two different types of hybrid applications may one day make the difference between the simple artificial intelligence we use today and those that will one day produce highly intelligent machines of tomorrow.

IBM's Watson for example, already used in the health care industry, is capable of sifting through massive amounts of data, learning just about anything that could be used to diagnose, treat, and monitor patient care.

While it can absorb these incredible amounts of data, as far as the decision making process, there is still much left to be desired. It still has yet to grasp abstract ideas and concepts. It is incapable of knowing what a patient is or what kind of impact a drug could have on a particular patient.

In contrast, the Tesla AI, used in automobiles, contains powerful software with features supported by a huge integration of cellular connectivity. It is the means by which we can have self-driving cars and gives machines the ability to meter identify potential threats in the environment.

Advantages and Disadvantages

Hybrid applications are the next cutting edge advancement in machine learning. There are many reasons why people are beginning to take such a keen interest in them.

•They have an undefined development so they can be adjusted to work on a variety of platforms.

•They are easier to maintain because they work with only one codebase.

•They can be developed easily in a very short period of time

•They can be cross-platform so they are easy to scale on different platforms and be used on different devices.

•They are less expensive

•Their components are interactive

Still, while they have made incredible strides in advancing the field of machine learning, they are not perfect. There are still several areas where they need to grow more in order to be the principle tool to use in the future.

•They tend to operate much slower because they are more often based on web tech.

•They have a poor UX. They are not yet capable of giving the user a full native experience.

Chapter 11: Where Do We Go From Here?

We have already established how wonderful it is and what it can do today. What's even more amazing is what it will be able to do in the future. Yes, the future looks very bright for so many reasons. Of course, there are many predictions (probably created by machine learning) of what we can expect, but chances are when the next evolution has passed, we'll probably all be utterly surprised, standing on the sidelines muttering, "I didn't know machines could do that!"

But what are the predictions for the future? What do we know now that we can confidently keep a watchful eye out for?

•Quantum Computing: Right now, machine learning is mostly in the field of problem solving. They manipulate and classify data at incredible speeds. In the future, quantum computers will be better equipped to manipulate high-dimensional vectors. They will accomplish this by using the hybrid training methods. By utilizing a blend of supervised and unsupervised algorithms, there will be a huge increase in the number of vectors resulting in a highly impressive rate of speed.

•Improved Unsupervised Algorithms: Their ability to discover hidden patterns in data on its own and self-learning techniques make it possible for unsupervised learning to be utilized more fully in the future. Machines of the future will be built smarter and mostly unsupervised.

•Collaborative Learning: They will have an enhanced ability to use other computational entities in a collaborative manner. This will allow them to produce better results than what is already being achieved now.

•Deeper Personalization: In the future, machines will know much more about you personally. While we may think this is very annoying and an invasion of our privacy, the feeble attempts used today will be greatly enhanced. Those frustratingly inaccurate recommendations will be a thing of the past, ending our frustrations with the whole process after all.

•Cognitive Services: No doubt, we will see many more intelligent features appear in even the most every day machines. Computer scientists are already working on emotion detection systems, speech recognition, vision recognition, and so much more.

No doubt, you will be able to think of many more possibilities for machine learning in the future, but as I said before, there is a good chance that the majority of the world will be surprised at what will come out.

Chapter 12: The Beginning Of Data Science

What is Data Science?

As we have already established in the introduction that data science is the core of most industries, and all around the globe, currently. Enjoying its position as the hot and most trendy topic of time, data science has made businessmen turn their heads in its direction. So, you may be wondering by now about the true nature of this term, 'data science'. Let us learn all about the basics of data science through this chapter.

In its simplest terms, data science is an interdisciplinary field of study that deals with a colossal amount of structured and unstructured data employing the latest techniques, tools and methods to discover new patterns, thresh out meaningful information, and help making important and intricate business decisions. Moreover, it makes use of complicated machine learning algorithms to create and modify predictive models.

The Data Science Lifecycle

There are five stages of Data science's life cycle:

1. Capture: The main purpose of the first stage is to get the raw material. In this process, data is the raw product. So we will accumulate data first. If you do not have massive data, you cannot proceed to the next steps.

In this stage, you can collect raw structured and unstructured data. You require a Technical skillset like MySQL to obtain the data.

Furthermore, if you are a beginner, you may use Microsoft Excel to collect data and then later convert it into usable data. You can also connect to websites' web servers to obtain data like Facebook and Twitter. Using their web API and then crawling out data are helpful. This stage includes:

- Data acquisition

- Data entry

- Signal reception

2. Maintain: The second stage is also known as the scrubbing stage. In this stage, unnecessary data is filtered that is irrelevant to the analysis. In the maintenance stage, it is necessary to do the following:

- Warehousing

- Cleansing

- Staging

- Processing

- Architecture of data

You have to convert the data from one format to another. Then, you need to merge it all into a standardized format. The second stage is known for transforming the raw information into usable data.

3. Process: In the third stage, the following important things are done:

- Mining

- Summarizing

- Clustering

- Analyzing

Data scientists analyze the patterns and explore the ranges and preferences of the data to determine its effectiveness in predictive analysis.

4. Data Modeling: It is the most important stage of the lifecycle in which all the data modeling is done. Some data scientists believe that it is the real magic.

The prepared data is used to organize the desired output in this process. The following steps are included:

1st Step: Choosing an appropriate machine learning algorithm for the model is required according to the type of data received.

2nd Step: Tuning the hyperparameters of the chosen model is performed to get the best results.

3rd Step: The accuracy and relevance of the model is evaluated.

5. Communication and Model deployment: It is the last stage in which the analyzed data is put into readable charts and graphs. Good and effective communication must be used to deliver the model results to stakeholders.

Most of the stakeholders are not interested in algorithms for the model. They are excited to know how your data model will drive the business world forward.

You might have listened to people around you using the terms machine learning, artificial intelligence with data science.

Though subtle, there is a difference among these three terms. It is important first to learn to distinguish the three terms and learn their peculiarities.

1. Artificial Intelligence: This term refers to getting a computer to imitate the behavior of humans.

2. Data Science: This is an umbrella category of artificial intelligence; it incorporates scientific methods and data analysis to get meaning and useful insight from data.

3. Machine learning: This term is another subcategory of artificial intelligence; it uses techniques that allow computers to observe and analyze the data and then carry out artificial intelligence applications. This term will be further discussed in the next chapter.

Data Science is the core foundation to learning

❏ Machine Learning

❏ Artificial Intelligence (A.I)

❏ Advanced-Data Analytics

❏ Advanced Statistics

We have already learned about the first two terms; now let us discover the other two.

1. Advanced-Data Analytics:

In the simplest terms, advanced data analytics is a term which includes all the high-level tools and methods to help you squeeze out the most information out of data. Advanced data analytics also has predictive power which can help you forecast events and trends. The predictive capability can be of great help to organizations as they can analyze future trends in the business and eradicate all possible risks.

Data mining is a vital aspect of advanced data analytics. In this automated process, usable information is extracted from large amounts of raw data.Advanced data analytics is a vast combination of analytical methods which aids businesses in finding and analyzing data trends by making use of data-driven statistics. These techniques include machine learning, data mining, forecasting, visualization, cluster analysis.

Businesses extract the most out of these advanced data analytics techniques because it strengthens their perspective and planning approach. Moreover, it improves their forecast and helps them in making better decisions. Such techniques help develop agility in business actions. Last but not the least, such methods reduce the risk of frauds and other collateral damages.

SOME FAMOUS EXAMPLES OF DATA SCIENCE

1. STREAMING SERVICES: All of us, in the current times, make use of online services. You stream online videos, movies and songs, but have you ever wondered the

engine behind these huge streaming services like Netflix, Hulu, or Spotify?

You might not know but data science plays the key role in bringing more happy customers to these online platforms by making their experience worthwhile. Data science gives the streaming businesses a vivid analysis of consumers' taste and experience in the form of charts and graphs. After having better information about the consumers' choice, the services are molded in a way that brings in more customer attraction.

Through use of data science, machine learning, and deep learning, online movie platforms like Netflix have grown exponentially. Netflix, despite its competition in the market, is able to secure most viewers through subscription method and account sharing technique. Established for years, this huge streaming business has gathered heaps of data about its consumers. You might be surprised to hear that the data is about the age, gender, place of living, and the tastes of the customers; the list goes even longer. Through gathering this individualistic data, Netflix provides services to each customer according to his own taste. Now you might be able to answer how Netflix gives you recommendations that just suit your preferences. So, before you even finish watching a movie, Netflix dives into your brain, and then offers the best movie you might like to see next.

We have data that suggests there is different viewing behavior depending on the day of the week, the time of day, the device, and sometimes even the location.

- Reed Hastings (CEO Netflix)

You must be wondering how Netflix and other streaming businesses collect, analyze and then utilize this vast data to help generate useful insights about the consumers and give out better results. Streaming services use various algorithms and mechanisms to make use of the heaps of data it has collected.

Near Real-Time Recommendations Engine is one such tool. The ratings that each individual gives on Netflix is added to the collection of Big Data stored in their database. Using these ratings and comments and using key learning algorithms, a fixed pattern is generated which is separate for each individual. It is because everyone's taste is unique, the pattern formed is also unique. So, the recommendation system suggests a preferable list of videos, songs or movies to watch.

"Netflix will know everything. Netflix will know when a person stops watching it. They have all of their algorithms and will know that this person watched five minutes of a show and then stopped. They can tell by the behavior and the time of day that they are going to come back to it, based on their history."

- Mitchell Hurwitz

Metaflow, Polynote, Metacat, Druid, and use of Python have made these online streaming services much more compatible and customer-friendly.

2. ECOMMERCE BUSINESS AND DATA SCIENCE

There are some amazing ways in which data science is changing, improving the world of ecommerce. Popular online shopping sites like Amazon and eBay keep a record of all the clicks you make on their sites and gather data of your shopping taste and experience. Using data science, these sites give personalized product recommendations.

Amazon is an example of this, 'Amazon Personalize' to generate individual product recommendations to ease customers and to increase sales. It has been calculated that 35% of revenue comes from Amazon's recommendation engine. According to a Barilliance report, 31% of revenue is generated through recommendation engines in the worldwide eCommerce industry.

3. HEALTHCARE AND DATA SCIENCE

Data science has made medical Image Analysis a crucial part of healthcare. Whether doctors need to check for tumors, or perform organ delineation, data science technology comes to the rescue. Methods like Deep Learning are used to find best ways to carry out tasks like lung texture classification.

Data science has helped scientists to improve their research in genetics and genomics. Scientists are using data science techniques to find the impact of DNA on human health and the relationship between drug response, diseases and genetics. Moreover, it helps combine different data with genomic data to help in the disease research, this can in turn help the scientists to analyze the genetic issues in reaction to different drugs and diseases.

The financial costs, lab tests, and the waiting time are factors which make drug development take years. However, data science and machine learning has made this process quicker. Screening of drug products in the start or the prediction of success rate are processes which take too much time. However, data science, through advanced mathematical modeling and other forecasting algorithms has made the process much more efficient and accurate.

WHY SHOULD YOU LEARN DATA SCIENCE?

1. Data Science is the career of tomorrow

With technology increasing by leaps and bounds, more and more industries, all over the world, are becoming data-driven. Data science has successfully made its place unchallenged in the coming future. The engine behind this evolving technology is the use of data science in almost all economies, institutions and businesses. By understanding global patterns, consumers' choice and emerging trends, data science has made the future of businesses more secure than ever. Many companies who have not yet switched to data science methods completely, have instead made small data science units to work on analytics. You might be surprised to hear that it is predicted that data science platforms will reach approximately 178 billion USD by the year 2025. So, the world of tomorrow is surely the world of data science.

There is a high demand for data scientists with an ever-increasing scope of data science. The reason is obvious. When big industries continue to generate more data, there is a high demand for data scientists to analyze both structured and unstructured data. Data scientists are also required in assisting the business companies in making smarter decisions and creating better and satisfactory products for the customers.

In the world of data science, it has become increasingly important to possess data literacy. We must learn the process of transforming the raw data into usable and meaningful products. Also, we should learn the methods and requirements to analyze and then draw useful insight from that data. Most of the job roles, in current times, require data handling as the main skill.

2. Data science is one of the most lucrative careers you can opt for

A Glassdoor study revealed that the average salary for a data scientist is $117,345 which is above the national average of $44,564. In even simpler terms, as a data scientist you can make 163% more than the national average salary. Now, you may know why being a data scientist can earn you success, fame and lots of money. The reality is that currently there is a scarcity of data Scientists and this is the reason there is a huge income bubble.

The learning curve of data science is quite steep because this interdisciplinary field requires a person to have knowledge and proficiency in various fields like Statistics, Mathematics, and Computer Science. Therefore, the market value of a data scientist is very high. Adding to the value, the pay scale of a data scientist is way above other IT and management sectors. However, one thing to keep in mind is that the salary of data scientists is just the proportional amount of work that they should put in. Data science is not just a simple field; it requires skills and hard work.

As a data scientist, you can always expect the most prestigious position in the company. Data scientists are relied upon by the company to make them steer into the right direction and help them make data-driven decisions. Not only this, the role of the Data scientist depends on the specialization of his employer company. For example – A commercial industry will require a data scientist to analyze their sales.

3. Basic Data science skills are important for personal use.

It is not that data science only helps those looking for jobs. In our daily routines, owning some basic data science skills can make our lives easier. You must be aware of online shopping. Are you? The famous Amazon earned billions during the pandemic as the online shopping trend skyrocketed. While shopping online, it is important to analyze the maximum, minimum and average price of an item from all online retailers, which can be done only if you know how to analyze sales data. Using this kind of data analysis, you can understand if you are paying too much for an item or not.

Teachers can better analyze the test scores of their students by using data science techniques. I use my data science knowledge to build models for personal use such as a home buying recommender system (to predict housing price based on predictors such as a number of rooms, square footage, age of the house, zip code, etc.), mortgage

calculator, etc.

4. Generate side income using Data science.

Generating side income through data science is no dream now. There are many ways you can earn additional money if you have a data science background by opting for freelancing, tutoring, teaching or blogging. In the beginning, I earned little money, $2 per month on my data science articles. Now, I earn $600 a month from my articles, certainly not house rent yet, but quite a good subsidiary income, especially as it is generated from something I love doing. No success can be gained from shortcuts; Data science is a field that can earn you lots of money, but it never guarantees overnight success. So, learn some basics of data science and start earning money.

Regardless, the ideas I'm about to suggest would certainly help you upskill, earn a good side income as a data scientist, and most importantly, be your own boss.

- Writing articles

- Participating in Kaggle competitions

- Doing freelance work

- Teaching

- Starting a YouTube Channel

5. Data Science will help you earn problem-solving skills.

Problem solving is a skill not easy to learn; it is a step wise process which will first help you learn to deal with smaller problems and then the bigger ones. Solving problems will distill greater confidence in you, and make you progress in life. Data science, python and machine learning teaches you the flair of problem solving. The power to think analytically and approach problems in the right way is a skill that's always useful, not just in the professional world, but in everyday life as well.

Problem solving technique also helps you believe in your ability to think mathematically and analytically. Problem-solving develops mathematical power. It gives students the tools to apply their mathematical knowledge to solve hypothetical and real-world problems.

6. Python and Data Science are in crazy demand.

If you are applying for a data-related job, then having Python with data science on your CV can give you a huge boost. In today's age, it is very rare that individuals have both python and data science skills; it is either Python or Data Science. So, if you have skills in both the fields, then it can give you an edge in the job market, and will make you stand out from other competitors.

HOW TO SET UP YOUR DATA SCIENCE ENVIRONMENT?

Before we move on to the step wise process of the data science environment, we need to learn what a data science environment is. It is the collection of relevant software and hardware in which the program executes. For example, if you are running a videogame with an intensive and intricate software on your outdated computer, then it is highly probable that your computer will slow down, or in worst cases, crash. It is because the environment which suited the video game was not provided by your computer.

1. Python and The Anaconda Package Management System.

Python is the top language used for data science and one of the fastest growing among all programming languages. It is believed that python's popularity owes to the ease with which it can be learned. In this section, we will use the Python programming language to solve data science problems. Also, we will look at the software and hardware requirements and the complete installation and setup details.

Software Requirements: For the best student experience, we recommend the following hardware configs.

● OS: Windows 7 SP1 64-bit, WIndows 8.1

64-bit or Windows 10 64-bit, Ubuntu Linux,

or the latest version of OS X

● Browser: Google Chrome/Mozilla Firefox

Latest Version

- Notepad++/Sublime Text as IDE (this is optional, as you can practice everything using jupyter Notebook on your browser)

- Python 3.4+ (latest is PYTHON 3.7) installed from https://python.org)

- Python Libraries as needed (Jupyter, Numpy, Pandas, Matplotlib and so on)

❏ Hardware Requirements: For the best student

experience, we recommend the following hardware

configs

- Processor: Intel Core i5 or equivalent

- Memory: 4 GB RAM

- Storage: 35 GB available space

Installation and Setup: Before you start this book make sure you have installed the anaconda environment as we will be using the Anaconda

distribution of python.

• Installing Anaconda: Install Anaconda by the following instruction:

• You must install offline copies of both docs.anaconda.com and enterprise-docs.anaconda.com by installing the conda package anaconda-docs:

conda install anaconda-docs

•You must install offline copies of documentation for many of Anaconda's open-source packages by installing the conda package anaconda-oss-docs:

conda install anaconda-oss-docs

•Qt and other packages released after Anaconda Distribution 5.1 (February 15th, 2018) may not work on macOS 10.9, so it may be necessary to not update certain packages beyond this point.

●Install Anaconda to a directory path that does not contain spaces or unicode characters.

●Do not install as Administrator unless admin privileges are required.

●If you did not download to your Downloads directory, replace ~/Downloads/ with the path to the file you downloaded.

●We recommend you accept the default install location. Do not choose the path as /usr for the Anaconda/Miniconda installation.

EXCLUSIVE FOR OUR READERS

Discover the blueprint in getting job market ready, overcome imposter syndrome, ace your data science interviews and land your first Data Science/Data Analyst job less than 3 months.

Chapter 13: What Is Machine Learning?

As we have established it before, most people confuse machine learning with data science, or even often, some call it a subcategory of data science, but for beginners, this introduction to machine learning can prove to be a little misleading. To put it in a few simple words, machine learning deals with building models of data.

Mathematical models are built in order to better and deeply understand data and decode it in all possible and useful ways. Models are located with different tunable parameters and then the program is made to 'learn' from the data. Models are first fitted to a seen data. After that it is used to analyze and predict the trends in the new data.

There are two major categories of machine learning to which you should be familiar at this stage.

1. Supervised Learning: In this category, relationships between measured features of data and some labels related to the data are modeled. Once model determining is done, the information can attach labels to new and unfamiliar data. This category is further divided into classification and regression tasks. In classification, labels are separate categories whereas in regression, labels are continuous quantities.

2. Unsupervised Learning: In this category, features of a data set are modeled without a reference to any label. This type of learning is often described as 'letting the dataset speak for itself.' Clustering and Dimensionality reduction are two subdivisions of unsupervised learning. In clustering, algorithms classify distinct clusters of data whereas in reduction, algorithms look for more brief representations of data.

There is also semi-supervised learning which, as the name suggests, falls somewhere between supervised and unsupervised learning. It comes handy when there are unidentified labels.

MACHINE LEARNING VS DATA SCIENCE

Before we move on to the details of machine learning, it is important to learn the key differences between the two terms: data science and machine learning.

Data science: It is an interdisciplinary field of study which takes a scientific approach to extract useful insight from the data. Data scientists need to be equipped with a unique combination of skills and experience. For example, one must be fluent in programming languages like Python and R; one must have knowledge of statistical methods, a deep understanding of database architecture, and most of all, knowledge and practice to apply this understanding and skills to real-world problems. As it is quite useless to have all the experience of data science without having any knowledge of how to incorporate it in a real-world situation.

With all its glory and supremacy, data science has certain limitations as well. As the functioning of data science purely depends on data, if the data is messy, small and incorrect, it can waste a lot of time. It will create models that generate meaningless and ambiguous results. Moreover, if the data does not sense the real reason behind variation, data science is useless.

Machine learning: It refers to various methods and tools employed by data scientists that permit computers to 'learn' from data. These methods generate results which perform exceptionally well without the need for programming rules.

Machine learning creates a useful model through testing various solutions against the given data and then searching the best solution for the problem. Therefore, problems which are highly labor intensive for us are taken good care of by machine learning. In a very efficient and reliable manner, machine learning can make predictions, and upon those predictions, make the best decision even of most complex issues.

This is the reason that most of the industries are now switching to machine learning as their main drive. Due to its vast possibilities, machine learning has the potential to even rescue endangered lives by solving critical problems in healthcare organizations. Machine learning algorithms have successfully cut many organizations' big costs by making useful decisions to solve problems.

However, there are certain limitations to machine learning as well. Even though its algorithms are quite useful in producing useful insights, we may still require programmers who can enhance the algorithms to make them solve newer problems. Also, in some cases, if we add machine learning to a problem that could be solved by traditional methods, it can complicate it further instead of solving it the simpler way.

One thing to keep in mind is that data science is a very vast term including many branches, and machine learning is one of its branches. Though not allowed to be mixed or interchanged, these two terms are related to a degree where data science is the umbrella term for machine learning. However, both have separate qualities and functions and both require a distinct skillset. Now let us look at the skills required in both machine learning and data science.

www.ingramcontent.com/pod-product-compliance
Lightning Source LLC
Chambersburg PA
CBHW071151050326
40689CB00011B/2073